(Quebec) Montréal, Charles Glackmeyer

Appendix to the charter and by-laws of the city of Montreal

containing amendments to the charter and by-laws passed since the last publication of the municipal laws in 1865

(Quebec) Montréal, Charles Glackmeyer

Appendix to the charter and by-laws of the city of Montreal
containing amendments to the charter and by-laws passed since the last publication of the
municipal laws in 1865

ISBN/EAN: 9783744740555

Printed in Europe, USA, Canada, Australia, Japan

Cover: Foto ©ninafisch / pixelio.de

More available books at **www.hansebooks.com**

APPENDIX

TO THE

CHARTER AND BY-LAWS

OF THE

CITY OF MONTREAL

CONTAINING

AMENDMENTS TO THE CHARTER AND BY-LAWS

PASSED SINCE THE LAST PUBLICATION

OF THE

MUNICIPAL LAWS

IN 1865.

COMPILED

BY

CHARLES GLACKMEYER

CITY CLERK.

Montreal
LA MINERVE STEAM PRESS, 16, ST. VINCENT STREET.

1870

PART FIRST.

AMENDMENTS

TO

THE CITY CHARTER

AND

OTHER ACTS OF THE LEGISLATURE

RELATING TO

THE CITY OF MONTREAL.

AMENDMENTS TO CHARTER.

(29 VICTORIA, CAP. 58.)

An act to explain certain enactments of the Acts of incorporation of the City of Montreal, and for other purposes.

[*Assented to* 18*th September*, 1865.]

WHEREAS doubts have arisen as to the true intent and meaning of the requirements of the forty-ninth section of the Act of incorporation of the City of Montreal, fourteenth and fifteenth Victoria, chapter one hundred and twenty-eight, as to the validity of the proceedings adopted by the Council of the City of Montreal, at the special meetings thereof from the time of its incorporation to the present day: Therefore, Her Majesty, by and with the advice and consent of the Legislative Council and Assembly of Canada, enacts and declares as follows: {Preamble. 14, 15 V. c. 128.}

1. All special meetings convened by the order of the Mayor or alderman in pursuance of the power granted in the said forty-ninth section, may be so called and convened by the order of the Mayor or alderman, by verbal or written intimation or notice to the city clerk, who thereupon shall issue the summons to the members of the said Council in the manner prescribed by the said forty-ninth section: {How special meetings of the City Council shall be called.}

2. All special meetings of the said Council called {Special meet-

AMENDMENTS TO CHARTER.

ings on requisition of members.

upon a requisition signed by five or more members of the said Council, in case of absence of the Mayor of the said city, or of his sickness, or his refusal to call the same, shall be deemed and considered a sufficient notice to authorize the city clerk to issue the summons to the members of the Council in the manner prescribed by the said section;

Special meetings heretofore called as above provided declared to have been legally called

3. All special meetings of the said Council heretofore called and convened by the Mayor or by an alderman, or by a requisition signed by five or more members of the said Council without any special notice signed by them or any of them to the said city clerk, requiring him to issue his summons in the form prescribed in the said forty-ninth section, shall be held and taken to have been so called and convened legally and in accordance with the requirements of the said forty-ninth section; Provided

Proviso: as to pending cases.

always, that nothing herein contained shall affect or prejudice the claims of any person or persons concerned in any proceeding, suit or instance now pending in the Superior Court of the District of Montreal, wherein the validity of certain proceedings of the said Council of the City of Montreal is called in question;

Recital. 27, 78 V. c. 60 s. 33.

2. And whereas it is enacted in and by the thirty-third section of the Act passed in the twenty-seventh and twenty-eighth years of Her Majesty's Reign, chapter sixty, "that any proprietor in the second, third and fourth sections of Notre-Dame street aforesaid, whose property, or any portion of whose property, is required for the said improvement, who may be desirous of anticipating the time fixed for carrying out the said improvement in front of his property, may do so, by amicable arrangement, at

AMENDMENTS TO CHARTER.

any time before the confirmation and homologation of the report of the said commissioners for the section of the said street in which such proprietor is interested, or after the confirmation and homolagation of the said report, by an acceptance of the terms or price set upon his property in the said. report;" but no provision is made to enable the Corporation of the said city to provide the necessary funds to meet the payment of the amount awarded in such cases, it is therefore enacted, that whenever any proprietor in the second, third or fourth sections of Notre Dame street, may desire to avail himself of the privilege conferred upon him by the said thirty-third section, by anticipating the time fixed for carrying out the widening of the said street in front of his property, such proprietor shall be bound to give a written notice of such his intention to the said corporation; and it shall be the duty of the said corporation to deposit, in the hands of the prothonotary of the Superior Court, within fifteen days from and after the said notice, the amount of the price and compensation which shall have been set upon the said property by the Commissioners. *Case of proprietor desiring to anticipate time fixed for widening the street provided for.*

3. And whereas it is expedient to simplify the procedure before the Recorder's Court in prosecutions instituted against parties selling spirituous, vinous or fermented liquors without license: it is hereby enacted that the said prosecutions before the said Court may henceforth be instituted either by a writ of summons or by warrant, as provided in and by chapter one hundred and three of the Consolidated Statutes of Canada, in relation to summary convictions before Justices of the Peace. *Proceedings in cases of sales of liquor without license simplified.*

4. For and notwithstanding anything contained *Oral evidence*

8 AMENDMENTS TO CHARTER.

may be given in such cases, and not reduced to writing. in the forty-seventh section of chapter six of the Consolidated Statutes for Lower Canada, it shall not be necessary, hereafter, to reduce the depositions of the witnesses in the said prosecutions before the said Recorder's Court, to writing, and to file the same of record in the cause, but the proof shall be made orally, as in cases of summary convictions.

Enforcement of penalty under sect. 3. 5. In default of the immediate payment of the penalty referred to in the third section of this Act, and such costs as are awarded to the prosecutor, the defendant shall be imprisoned under the warrant of the Recorder of the said City, for a period of not less than two months and not exceeding six months; but the defendant may, at any time, obtain his liberation from such imprisonment, by making full payment of the said penalty, and all costs, whether incurred upon or after conviction.

Recital. 6. And whereas delays and obstructions have occurred in dealing with cases and suits cognizable by the Recorder's Court of the said city, by reason of doubts which were raised as to the power of the Clerk of the said Recorder's Court to conduct the said cases and suits, it is hereby declared and enacted as follows :

Clerk of Recorder's Court to conduct cases for the City. The said clerk of the Recorder's Court is authorized and vested with all the necessary powers, and it is his duty to conduct in behalf and in the name of the plaintiffs or prosecutors, when such plaintiffs or prosecutors are, or shall be, the Corporation of the said City of Montreal, all cases and suits cognizable by and within the jurisdiction of the said Court.

Additional loan for drainage authorized. 7. For the purpose of completing the drainage of the said city, and for that purpose only, it shall be lawful for the said corporation to borrow, over and above the amount of the loan which the said corpo-

AMENDMENTS TO CHARTER.

ration is authorized to raise in and by the provisions of the thirty-fifth section of the Act passed in the twenty-seventh and twenty-eighth years of Her Majesty's Reign, chapter sixty, such sum or sums of money, not exceeding seventy-five thousand dollars, as the said corporation may find it necessary or expedient to borrow, for the extension and completion of the drainage of the said city.

8. For the purpose of establishing and erecting a Drill Shed and Armory in the said city, and acquiring the necessary site therefor, and for these purposes only, it shall be lawful for the said corporation to effect a special loan not exceeding seventy-five thousand dollars to be designated *The Drill Shed Loan.* <small>Loan for Drill Shed and Armory.</small>

9. The said corporation is hereby authorized to borrow a sum not exceeding two hundred thousand dollars for the purpose of providing an additional rising main water pipe and further to extend the Water Works of the said city and for no other purpose. <small>Loan for water works.</small>

10. It shall be lawful for the corporation of the said city to issue, under the hand of the Mayor and the seal of the said corporation, debentures or corporation bonds to the amount of the respective sums which the said Corporation is empowered to borrow, in and by the three next preceding sections, payable twenty-five years after the date of the issue thereof respectively, and bearing interest payable semi-annually on the first day of May and November in each and every year, and at a rate not exceeding six per centum per annum, and all such debentures may be issued from time to time, at such periods and for such amounts as shall be deemed expedient, and they may have coupons annexed to them for <small>Issue of Debentures authorized: form, interest, &c.</small>

the half-yearly interest payable on them, which coupons, being signed by the Mayor or Treasurer of the said corporation, shall be respectively payable to the bearer thereof when the half-yearly interest therein mentioned becomes due, and shall on payment thereof, be delivered up to the said corporation ; and the possession of any such coupons by the corporation shall be *prima facie* evidence that the half year's interest therein mentioned has been paid according to the tenor of such debentures or bonds; and as well the interest as the principal thereof are and shall be secured to the general funds of the said corporation.

Loans may be effected in or out of the Province, &c.
11. The amount which the said corporation is empowered to borrow by the next preceding sections, may be borrowed either in this Province or elsewhere ; and the principal sum and the interest thereon as aforesaid, may be made payable either in this Province or elsewhere, and either in sterling money or the currency of this Province, or in that of the place where the same shall be payable.

Sinking Fund and Treasurer's duty with respect to it.
12. It shall be the duty of the treasurer of the said city, before the quarterly meeting of the council of the said city, in the month of September, in the year one thousand eight hundred and sixty-six, and in each year thereafter, to take from and out of the annual revenues and funds of the corporation of the said city (from whatever source arising), and before the payment of any appropriation whatsoever of the said revenues or funds, a sum of money equal to two per cent, on the debt or debts created under the authority of this Act, and under the authority of the first section of the Act passed in the twenty-fifth year of Her Majesty's Reign, chapter forty-four, and of the thirty-fourth and thirty-fifth sections of the

Act passed in the twenty-seventh and twenty-eighth years of Her Majesty's Reign, chapter sixty; which said sum of money the said city treasurer shall keep apart of all other monies, to be invested and applied, under the orders of the said council, solely and exclusively as a sinking fund, towards the extinction of the said debt or debts, in the same manner and under the same formalities as prescribed in and by the sixth section of the Act passed in the sixteenth year of Her Majesty's Reign, chapter twenty-six, and generally all the provisions contained in the said sixth section of the said last cited Act, shall apply to the sinking fund established under the authority of this Act, except only in so far as they are inconsistent with this Act. *Investment and application of such Fund.*

13. This Act shall be deemed a Public Act. *Public Act.*

AMENDMENTS TO CHARTER.

(29-30, VICTORIA, CAP. 56.)

An Act to amend the provisions of several Acts relating to the City of Montreal, and for other purposes.

[Assented to 15th August, 1866.]

Preamble

WHEREAS the Corporation of the City of Montreal have, by their petition, asked for several changes to be made in the provisions of the Acts of incorporation of the said city, and it is expedient to accede to the prayer contained in the said petition: Therefore, Her Majesty, by and with the advice and consent of the Legislative Council and Assembly of Canada, enacts as follows:

Time allowed for election of Mayor, &c., altered.

1. From and after the passing of this Act, the delay granted to persons qualified to vote at the election of Mayor and Councillors of the said city, to produce and deposit their certificates of qualification to that effect, and vote, shall be from nine o'clock in the forenoon until five o'clock in the afternoon of the last four juridical days in the month of February of each year.

Proprietors to vote for Councillors in every ward where they own real estate, &c.

2. Every male person being the owner of real estate in more than one ward of the said city, and every male person being the occupant of an office or place of business in one of the said wards, and being the occupant of a dwelling-house or the owner of real estate in any other ward or wards, shall have the right to vote, for the election of Coun-

cillors only, in any ward wherein he owns real estate, or occupies a dwelling-house, as also in the ward wherein such person shall keep an office or place of business; and such person shall be inscribed in the voters' list for each of the said wards; provided such person be otherwise qualified and within the requirements of the law.

Proviso.

3. The seventh and eighth sections of the Act passed in the fifteenth year of Her Majesty's Reign, (fourteenth and fifteenth Victoria chapter one hundred and twenty-eight,) are hereby amended in so far as they enable the Mayor, Aldermen and Councillors of the said city to qualify on personal estate; and henceforth the Mayor and Aldermen shall not be capable of being elected, unless they are, during the six months immediately preceding the day of their nomination, seized and possessed, as proprietors, of real estate within the limits of the said city, of the value of one thousand pounds, currency, after payment, or deduction of their just debts; and the Councillors shall not be capable of being elected, unless they are, during the six months immediately preceding the day of their nomination, seized and possessed, as proprietors, of real estate within the limits of the said city, of the value of five hundred pounds, said currency, after payment or deduction of their just debts; and the form of oath inserted in the thirty-ninth section of the Act fourteenth and fifteenth Victoria, chapter one hundred and twenty-eight, is hereby amended by striking out therefrom all that relates to personal estate.

Qualification of Members of Council to be on real estate only.

Mayor and Aldermen.

Councillors.

Form of oath altered.

4. No person shall enter upon office as Mayor, Alderman or Councillor of the said city, unless he shall have previously deposited and lodged in the hands of the City Clerk, a declaration signed by

Declaration of qualification.

AMENDMENTS TO CHARTER.

himself, establishing the fact of his being qualified in accordance with the provisions of the next preceding section, and containing a detailed description of the real estate on which he qualifies himself.

If property on which a member has qualified changes hands, &c.

5. In case the Mayor or any Alderman or Councillor shall cede or make over, in any manner whatsoever, the real estate on which he shall have qualified himself, or shall mortgage or encumber the same, so as to affect the amount required for his qualification, it shall be lawful for any two electors duly qualified to vote at the election of the said Mayor, Alderman or Councillor respectively, to present a Petition to the Council of the said city, requiring the said Mayor, Alderman or Councillor, as the case may be, to produce the title of such other immovable property as he may qualify upon; failing which, his seat shall become vacant.

He must qualify on other property.

Person indebted for city taxes not eligible as members of Council.

6. No person shall be capable of being elected a member of the Council of the said city, who may be indebted to the said city for taxes, assessments or water rates (drain accounts or special assessments in cases of expropriation excepted) or is a party to, or interested in, any law suit or judicial process whatsoever, the amount of which shall exceed one hundred dollars currency and wherein the Corporation of the said city shall appear as plaintiff or defendant.

Other causes of disqualification.

7. Any member of the said Council who shall, directly or indirectly, become a party to, or security for, any contract or agreement to which the Corporation of the said city is a party, or shall derive any interest, profit or advantage from such contract or agreement, shall thereby become disqualified and lose his seat in the said Council.

Acting City Treasurer in certain cases.

8. In case of the absence of the City Treasurer by sickness or otherwise, the Mayor, for the time being,

AMENDMENTS TO CHARTER.   15

may appoint a person to act as such Treasurer during the said absence.

9. The thirty-eighth section of the said Act fourteenth and fifteenth Victoria, chapter one hundred and twenty-eight, is hereby repealed. <small>Sec. 38 of 14 and 15 Vic. cap. 128 repealed.</small>

10. At the quarterly meeting of the said Council to be held in the month of December next, one thousand eight hundred and sixty-six, the said Council shall elect, by a majority of votes, a person to be, and who shall be named the "Auditor for the City of Montreal," whose duties and attributions shall be prescribed by a by-law which the said Council is hereby authorized to pass; Provided always, that no member of the said Council, nor the city clerk, nor the assistant city clerk shall be capable of being elected Auditor as aforesaid; Provided also, that any vacancy in the office of Auditor may be filled by the said Council, by an election to be made in the manner prescribed by and in conformity with the provisions hereinbefore made, at any subsequent quarterly or special meeting. <small>Auditor to be elected by Council: duties. Proviso. Proviso.</small>

11. A majority in value of the proprietors interested in or subject to a special assessment may, by a declaration to that effect, to be signed by the said proprietors, object to the carrying out of any improvement, by submitting such declaration to the Commissioners named, for the purposes of the said improvement, by the court or any judge, as the case may be, two days at least before the day fixed on which to proceed with the valuation; and in that case, instead of proceeding with the valuation on the day appointed, the said Commissioners shall ascertain and determine, without any appeal, if, in reality, the signers of the said declaration constitute the majority in value of the said parties interested, (the <small>Majority of proprietors interested in any improvement may object to its being carried out, &c. Duty of Commissioners in such case.</small>

said value as set forth and established in and by the general assessment roll immediately preceding such declaration,) and if they find that such majority are opposed to the improvement, they shall report the fact to the Court or Judge, as the case may be, on the day appointed to receive their report of valuation, and the proceedings in expropriation shall *ipso facto* be annulled; if, on the contrary, the said Commissioners determine that a majority in value of the parties interested have not signed the said declaration, they shall appoint a day on which to proceed to determine the value of the real estate subject to expropriation, of which they shall give notice by publication in one newspaper in the French language, and one newspaper in the English language published in the said city.

Commissioners to make out special assesment in cases of local improvement

12. The twenty-second and twenty-fifth sections of the Act twenty-seventh and twenty-eighth Victoria, chapter sixty, are hereby repealed; and it is enacted that the said Commissioners, at the same time that they determine and fix upon the amount of the price, indemnity or compensation for each and every the pieces or parcels of ground required by the Corporation of the said City, for purposes of improvements, shall also proceed to assess and apportion, in such manner as to them may appear most reasonable, the price or compensation, indemnity or damage and cost of such expropriation or improvement, in whole or in part, conformably to the resolution of the said Council, upon all and every the pieces or parcels of land or real estate, which shall have been benefited or may hereafter be benefited by such improvement; and the said Commissioners shall have the exclusive power or privilege to determine what pieces or parcels of land or real estate

AMENDMENTS TO CHARTER.

shall have been or may be benefited, and to what relative or comparative amount; and the said Commissioners shall, for the purposes of the said improvement, base their valuation upon the actual value of the said pieces or parcels of land or real estate, irrespective of buildings thereon erected, taking into account the size of the said pieces or parcels of ground or real estate and the benefit to be derived from the said improvement; and two of the said Commissioners shall have full power to act for the purposes of the said special assessment, in case of a diversity of opinion, and their decision shall have the same force and effect as if the three Commissioners had concurred therein. *On what the assessment shall be based.*

Two Commissioners may act.

13 The twenty-third section of the said Act twenty-seventh and twenty-eighth Victoria, chapter sixty, is hereby amended by striking out the words "along with a plan or map designating all and every the pieces or parcels of land or real estate subject to or liable for the said special assessment;" and by substituting the word "Comissioners" for the word "Assessors" wherever the latter word occurs; but the provisions contained in the two next preceding sections shall not apply to cases where the Commissioners shall have commenced the proceedings of expropriation at the time of the passing of this Act. *Sec. 23 of 27 & 28 V. Cap., 60, amended.*

14. When the Corporation of the said City, after having resolved to carry out an improvement, at the cost of the parties interested, in whole or in part, shall have acquired by amicable arrangement and without having recourse to proceedings in expropriation, all the pieces or parcels of ground required for the said improvement, (hypothesis under which, before the repeal of the sections of the said Act *Commissioners to be appointed to assess in cases, where the land is acquired by amicable arrangement.*

AMENDMENTS TO CHARTER.

twenty-seventh and twenty-eighth Victoria, chapter sixty hereby abrogated, the City Assessors were held to assess and apportion, without limitation as to time, the cost of the improvement upon the real estate benefited) the said Corporation shall, by a petition to be addressed to the Superior Court or to any Judge thereof, in vacation, cause to be appointed three Commissioners for the special purpose of making and determining the apportionment or special assessment to cover the cost of the said improvement, in whole or in part, as the case may be ; and the said Commissioners shall make such apportionment or special assesment in the manner specified in the foregoing sections ; nothing herein contained shall deprive any of the parties interested from availing themselves of any irregularity in the original proceedings, and of contesting the right of the said Corporation to make or cause such assesment to be made.

Rights saved.

Sec. 17 of 27 & 28 V. c. 60, amended.

15. The seventeenth section of the said Act, twenty-seventh and twenty-eighth Victoria, chapter sixty, is hereby amended, and hereafter all the powers conferred upon the Superior Court by the said section to call in the creditors and issue such orders as regards the distribution of the price or indemnity, shall be exercised with as much validity by any of the Judges of the said Court during the vacation and out of term.

Delay within which real estate may be sold for taxes.

16. The delay of five years, fixed by the seventy-fifth section of the Act fourteenth and fifteenth Victoria, chapter one hundred and twenty-eight, for the sale of real estate, in case of non payment of the assessments due thereon, is hereby reduced to two years.

Loan of $400,000 to pay all float-

17. And whereas it is expedient to make provisions for consolidating the floating debt of the said

AMENDMENTS TO CHARTER.

City and for placing the financial affairs of the said City on a better footing, by providing means for paying off the said debt, by means of a sinking fund: it is enacted that it shall be lawful for the said corporation to borrow, by and through the issue of debentures, in sums not less than five hundred dollars each, a sum not exceeding four hundred thousand dollars to pay off and extinguish the floating debt; and the provisions of the second section of the Act sixteenth Victoria, chapter twenty-six and of the twelfth section of the Act twenty-ninth Victoria, chapter fifty-eight, relating to the sinking fund, shall apply to the loan authorized by the present section. *ing debt, authorized.*

Certain provisions to apply.

18. It shall be lawful for the said corporation to borrow, by means of debentures to be issued for that purpose, in sums not less than five hundred dollars each, a sum of one hundred and seventy-five thousand dollars to be applied exclusively to the amelioration of the Water Works of the said city, a portion of which sum, viz: one hundred thousand dollars shall be specially applied to the extension of the reservoir, and seventy-five thousand dollars to provide against unforeseen accidents which may occur in the winter season, and for no other purposes; and the provisions of the second section of the Act sixteenth Victoria, chapter twenty-six, and of the twelfth section of the Act twenty-ninth Victoria, chapter fifty-eight in relation to a sinking fund shall apply to the loan authorized by the present section. *Loan of $175,000 for water works.*

What provisions to apply.

19. This Act shall be deemed a public Act. *Public Act.*

AMENDMENTS TO CHARTER.

(31, VICTORIA, CAP. 37.)

An Act to amend the acts relating to the Corporation of the City of Montreal, and for other purposes.

[*Assented to*, 24*th February*, 1868.]

Preamble.

WHEREAS, the corporation of the city of Montreal have, by their petition, asked for several changes to be made in the provisions of the acts of incorporation of the said city and that the said corporation are desirous of obtaining more ample powers to make certain alterations in the system followed in the issuing of bonds, their guarantee, and the payment of interest thereon, and of improving the financial condition of the said city by creating a consolidated fund to withdraw the bonds and debentures at present in circulation, and to extinguish and pay off the existing debt and converting it into bonds or securities which may be negociated to greater advantage, owing to the additional security they will offer to purchasers : Therefore, Her Majesty, by and with the advice and consent of the Legislature of Quebec, enacts as follows :

Montreal consolidated fund established.

1. A consolidated fund is hereby established for the city of Montreal, to be known as "the city of Montreal consolidated fund," which shall consist of stock or shares and debentures of one hundred dollars each, which the corporation of the said city may dispose of, from time to time, as opportunity offers, to an amount not exceeding five millions of dollars, current money of this province ; and the said stock or shares and debentures shall form three classes, under letters A, B, C, to be composed as follows :

Fund divided into 3 classes.

AMENDMENTS TO CHARTER.

1. Class A shall comprise the stock or shares to be known as "the Montreal water works stock," to the amount of three millions of dollars, current money of this province, which shall be applied towards the paying off and extinction of the debt incurred for, and in respect of the water works of the said city, and shall be secured by special mortgage and privilege and without the formality of registration at the registry office, on the real estate, buildings, machinery, apparatus, mechanism and works generally in connection with the water works department. *Class A.*

2. Class B. shall comprise the stock or shares to be known as "the Montreal public property stock," to the amount of one million dollars, current money of this province, which shall be applied towards the paying off and extinction of the debt incurred for, and in respect of, public property in the said city, and shall be secured by special mortgage and privilege, and without the formality of registration at the registry office, upon the public markets, fire and police stations, fire alarm telegraph and drill shed, including the land in connection therewith the old St. Ann's market property lying between McGill, William and College streets, and the public squares in the said city. *Class B.*

3. Class C. shall comprise the bonds or debentures to be known as "the Montreal terminable debentures," to the amount of one million of dollars, current money of this province, which shall be applied towards the paying off and extinction of the general debt of the said city, and shall be secured by a sinking fund, as hereinafter provided. *Class C.*

2. The shares or stock comprised in the two first classes, to wit: "the Montreal water works stock," *The shares in A and B shall be permanent*

AMENDMENTS TO CHARTER.

and "the Montreal public property stock," shall be permanent, in perpetuity and unredeemable; and the bonds or debentures of the third class, to wit: "the Montreal terminable debentures," shall be payable in twenty-five years from date; and upon all shares, stock or debentures of the three classes above mentioned, as forming the "city of Montreal consolidated fund," there shall be paid by the treasurer of the said city to each of the subscribers to the said consolidated fund, at the office of the said treasurer, at the city hall of the said city, a uniform interest at the rate of seven per cent every year, semi-annually, on the first day of May and the first day of November.

Certificate to be given to purchasers for shares.

3. Any person who shall subscribe for or purchase one or more shares in the said consolidated fund, shall receive from the treasurer of the said city a certificate to that effect, to be signed by the mayor of the said city, and sealed with the seal of the said city; which said certificate may be in the form of schedules number one and number two [as the case may be,] appended to the present act.

Shares may be realized.

4. It shall be lawful for the said corporation to negotiate the said shares, stock and debentures either in this province or elsewhere, and to pay the interest on the same either in sterling money or in the current money of this province, and to pay off class C, terminable debentures, in like manner.

Stock book.

5. It shall be the duty of the city treasurer to enregister, in a book to be kept for that purpose, all shares, stock and debentures to be negotiated by virtue of the preceding sections, as they are disposed of, and also the name of each individual, person, or firms of persons or corporations, who may have sub-

AMENDMENTS TO CHARTER.

scribed to any amount of the said shares, stock or debentures; and when such subscriber or subscribers shall transfer or make over his or their said shares to a third party, such transfer or cession may be made in the form of schedules number three and number four [as the case may be] appended to this act; and the same shall be entered or registered by the said treasurer in a distinct book or register to be kept by the said treasurer for that purpose, and to which access may be had by interested parties, on demand; and such subscriber or transferee last enregistered, as hereinbefore prescribed, shall be held to be *prima facie* the creditor of the amount of such shares, stock or debentures, and such shares, stock and debentures are and shall be transferable in the manner aforesaid. Transfer book; which will be *prima facie* proof.

6. Every year, on or before the thirty-first day of January, the city treasurer shall take from and out of the annual revenues and other funds of the said corporation, and before the payment of any appropriation whatsoever of the said revenues or funds, a sum of money equal to two per cent on the sum of one million dollars, current money of this province, which said sum of two per cent, every year, the said treasurer shall keep apart from all other moneys, to be invested and applied solely and exclusively as a sinking fund, towards the extinction of the debt created by the realization of the debentures under class C, known as the "Montreal terminable debentures," as hereinafter provided; and the said treasurer shall invest the sum thus set apart as a sinking fund in public securities, or bonds of the federal government of Canada, or the local government of Quebec, and not otherwise: provided however the said treasurer may, if deemed advisa- Sinking fund for the extinction of debentures under class C.

Sinking fund how invested.

AMENDMENTS TO CHARTER.

Duties imposed on treasurer by this section.

ble by the finance committee of the said corporation, pay off, from and out of the said sinking fund, any sum in deduction of the debt created by the "Montreal terminable debentures" towards the gradual extinction of such debt; and the said treasurer shall place before the city council, at its first quarterly meeting in the month of March of each year, a certificate signed by himself and countersigned by the mayor of the said city, to the effect that he has faithfully fulfilled the obligations imposed upon him by the present section of this act, and in default of his so doing the said city treasurer shall become and be liable to pay to the said corporation a fine of two thousand dollars, said currency, which said fine may be exacted in the same manner as all other fines imposed in and by the several statutes concerning the said corporation, and shall form part of the sinking fund aforesaid; and it shall be the duty of the auditor of the said city to submit to the said council annually a statement under oath showing whether the said treasurer has or has not fulfilled all the obligations imposed upon him by the present section.

Corporation shall retain a sum equal to the amount of its bonds now in circulation, which it may redeem or not.

7. The corporation of the said city shall at all times retain in their hands from and out of the "city of Montreal consolidated fund," a sum equivalent to the amount of their bonds, securities or debentures, then in circulation and issued in virtue of the several statutes concerning the said corporation; and it shall be lawful for the said corporation, with the said sum, to redeem the bonds, or debentures in circulation at maturity, or by agreement with the holders thereof, or to receive the same in exchange for shares, stock or debentures available in virtue of the present act, on such terms and conditions as may be agreed upon.

AMENDMENTS TO CHARTER. 25

8. The corporation of the said city are hereby empowered to employ and apply all sums of money now on hand and set apart, by and through their treasurer, to form sinking funds in pursuance of the several statutes by which the said corporation are authorized to borrow money for municipal purposes, and which at present constitute such sinking funds, to the payment and extinction of the bonds, securities, debentures, and of the debt of the city generally; and such sinking funds being rendered unnecessary by reason of the system inaugurated by the present act, the same are for the future discontinued and declared to be abolished. *Investment of sinking fund already created.*

EXPROPRIATION.

9. The eleventh and twelfth sections of the act passed in the twenty-ninth and thirtieth years of Her Majesty's reign, intituled: "An act to amend the provisions of several acts relating to the city of Montreal and for other purposes," are hereby explained and modified in manner and to the extent following:—the said commissioners, before proceeding with the valuation required by the said sections, shall begin by determining who are the parties interested in and to be specially assessed for the purpose of the proposed improvement, and draw up a report thereof, and give public notice of the same by an advertisement to be inserted during ten days in two English and two French daily newspapers published in the city of Montreal, and the said parties so notified who desire to oppose the said proposed improvement shall be bound to fyle their oppositions in the hands of the said commissioners, within three days from the date of the last insertion of the said advertisement, the said commissioners, *Sections 11, 12 of 29, 30 V. c. 57 modified. Duty of commissioners before assessing value.*

upon the fyling of the said oppositions, to proceed as mentioned in the said sections.

TAVERN CERTIFICATES.

Preamble.

10. Whereas, the council of the said city of Montreal have experienced serious difficulties in the fulfilment of the duties imposed upon them by law in reference to the granting of certificates for taverns, inns, hotels or other houses or places of public entertainment, and it is expedient to relieve the said council, from such responsibility, and for that purpose to amend chapter six of the consolidated statutes for Lower Canada ; it is therefore enacted that the powers conferred upon the said city council by sections nine, eleven and thirteen, of chapter six of the consolidated statutes for Lower Canada, concerning the confirmation or rejection of the certificates required to obtain a license, are henceforth conferred upon a board to be composed of the chairmen of the standing committees of the said council, who are hereby exclusively invested with all the rights and powers held to this day by the said council, concerning the said granting or rejection of tavern certificates.

Powers given by secs. 9, 11, 13 of c. 6, C. S. L. C. for granting tavern certificates transferred to chairmen of permanent committees.

11. All applications for certificates shall be lodged with the clerk of the said city, on or before the fifteenth day of March in each and every year and no later ; and each application aforesaid shall be accompanied by the sum of one dollar to defray the cost of advertising and other incidental expenses.

When such certificates shall be applied for.

12. It shall be the duty of the said board to consider the said applications for certificates, and to grant or reject the same, as they may see fit, and to close their labors on or before the fifteenth day of April following and not later, and they shall report

When applications shall be taken into consideration.

the result of their proceedings to the city clerk, which report shall be signed by a majority of the members of the said board, and their adjudication shall be final.

13. Immediately after the above mentioned report shall have been made, the clerk of the said city shall cause to be published, without delay, in the newspapers in which the advertisements of the corporation of the said city usually appear, a complete list of the applicants whose applications have been granted by the said board. *List of applications granted to be published.*

RECORDER'S COURT.

14. Whereas, as it is expedient to simplify the procedure of the recorder's court of the city of Montreal, with reference to enregistration of proceedings, judgments and convictions therein, it is hereby enacted that it shall not be necessary to enregister at full length the proceedings, judgments and convictions of the said court, but a roll only of the said judgment and one of convictions shall be duly kept by the clerk of the said court, wherein shall be set forth in the first case, the name of the defendant, the nature of the debt and the date of judgment, and in the second, the nature of the offence, the penalty and the date of conviction, and the notes of proceedings noted in the original summons or plaint shall be sufficient evidence thereof; provided that in cases when the defendant requests prior to the hearing of the case to have the proceedings entered as heretofore, the above provisions shall not apply. *More simple mode of recording the proceedings of the Court. Proviso.*

15. In all cases of persons tried for drunkenness before the said court, it shall not be necessary to take the affidavit or deposition in writing of the constable making the arrest. *In certain cases depositions need not be in writing.*

AMENDMENTS TO CHARTER.

CITY HALL LOAN.

Preamble.

16. And whereas, the premises now used in the said city of Montreal as a city hall, are inadequate to the proper working and administration of the municipal affairs, and do not offer sufficient security for the preservation of the city's archives and documents, and in consequence thereof, the corporation of the said city have acquired from the provincial government, by deed passed at the said city of Montreal, on the twenty-ninth day of June, one thousand eight hundred and sixty seven, before Théod. Doucet and colleague notaries, a lot of ground or real property situated within the limits of the said city, on the express condition that the said corporation shall construct on the said lot or real property a city hall, and shall not use the same for any other purposes, and that the said edifice shall be erected within five years from the date of such deed, and to enable the said corporation to fulfil their engagements as aforesaid, it is hereby enacted that the said corporation may effect a special loan *Loan of $250,000 and issue of bonds, to build a city hall.* to the amount of two hundred and fifty thousand dollars, current money of this province, to be known as "The City Hall Loan," for which the said corporation are authorized to issue, under the signature of the mayor and the seal of the said corporation, bonds or debentures to the amount of the said sum of two hundred and fifty thousand dollars, payable twenty-five years after the date of their issue, and bearing interest at the rate of seven per cent, every year, payable semi-annually on the first day of May *Nature and security of said bonds.* and the first day of November, and such bonds or debentures may be issued from time to time, for such period and for such amount as may be deemed

AMENDMENTS TO CHARTER.

expedient, and shall, as regards the principal as well as the interest, be secured by special mortgage and privilege, and without the formality of registration at the registry office by and upon the lot or land acquired as aforesaid, for a city hall, and also by and upon the buildings and works to be erected thereon; provided, however, the proceeds of the said bonds or debentures shall be applied and expended only for the purposes of the erection of a city hall on the lot of ground aforesaid, and not otherwise or elsewhere.

17. The amount which the corporation of the said city are authorized to borrow, in and by the preceding section, may be borrowed either in this Province, or elsewhere, in sterling money, or in the current money of this province, or in the current money of the place where made payable; and all the provisions contained in the fourth, fifth and sixth sections of the present act, regulating the issue of bonds and debentures, their registration and transfer, and the establishment of a sinking fund, under the responsibility of the treasurer of the said city, and his rights and obligations in that respect, shall apply also to the issuing, enregistering, transferring and payment of the bonds or debentures, the issue of which is authorized by the preceding section, and to the establishing of a sinking fund, at the rate of two per cent annually, on the said sum of two hundred and fifty thousand dollars, for the purpose of paying off the said loan. *Where the loan may be effected. Secs. 4. 5. 6, shall apply to said bonds.*

MISCELLANEOUS PROVISIONS.

18. In case any returning officer appointed by the council of the said city to preside at the nomination of candidates, at municipal elections, shall, from *Absence of returning officers at elections provided for.*

AMENDMENDS TO CHARTER.

illness or unavoidable absence or other cause, be unable to perform the duties devolving upon him, power is given to the clerk of the said city to appoint, from among the members of the said council, a substitute to preside at such elections in the place of such returning officer.

Extension of 27-28 V. c. 60, s. 27 as to street paving.

19. The powers conferred upon the council of the said city by the twenty-seventh section of the act twenty-seventh and twenty-eight Victoria, chapter sixty, in reference to dressed stone paving, flagstone or brick foot-paths or sidewalks, or grading, and the defraying of the cost thereof in whole or in part by means of an assessment, are extended to such other modes of paving as the said city council may adopt by resolution, such as wooden block, or Nicholson paving, asphalt, lava, or any other paving composition whatsoever.

How near to dwellings water pipes need be laid.

20. In all cases where a building is now, or shall hereafter be constructed within and at a distance from the line of the street, the corporation of the said city shall be held to lay the water distribution pipes to the line of the street only, and the said corporation shall have the right to exact the water rate from the proprietor of such building, although the latter shall fail or neglect to connect the said distribution pipe with his building.

By-law to prohibit keeping of pigs.

21 The council of the said city shall have power and authority to prohibit the rearing, keeping or feeding of pigs within the limits of the said city, or in such sections as the said council shall determine and to pass a by-law for that purpose, and may impose by such by-law a fine not exceeding twenty dollars, or an imprisonment not exceeding two months unless such fine be sooner paid, or may im-

pose such fine with the addition of the said imprisonment for the said offence, as may be deemed expedient.

22. All sections of any law contrary to the provisions of the present act, shall be and they are hereby repealed, but in so far only as they are inconsistent with the said provisions. *General repeal.*

SCHEDULE No. 1.

CITY OF MONTREAL CONSOLIDATED FUND.

Classes A or B.

PERMANENT STOCK.

CITY HALL,

Montreal. 18

CERTIFICATE No.

This is to certify that   *Form of certificate of shares in classes A and B.*
of   at the date hereof, is the
registered owner, in the books of the corporation of
the city of Montreal, of
shares, of one hundred dollars each, in all amounting to   of the
consolidated fund of the city of Montreal (as detailed in the margin hereof,) established under the authority of the act of the Legislature of Quebec, in the Dominion of Canada, passed on the
day of   18   , (Vic., chap.   ,)
intituled : " An act to amend the acts relating to the

AMENDMENTS TO CHARTER

Shares. Shares. Shares.

Class A—Montreal Water Works Stock, Class B—Montreal Public Property Stock. In all, as certified herein.

corporation of the city of Montreal and for other purposes."

Upon the amount of shares in the said permanent stock standing enregistered to the credit of the owners thereof, in the books of the corporation of the city of Montreal as aforesaid, the corporation of the mayor, aldermen and citizens of the said city will pay interest semi-annually, at the rate of seven per cent per annum, on the first days of May and November in each year.

Sealed with the seal of the corporation of the said city of Montreal—signed by the mayor—countersigned by the city clerk and enregistered in the books of the said corporation by the city treasurer of the said city, this   day of
               , 18 .

(L. S.)   Mayor,
                    City clerk.
Registered book   Folio
                                              City Treasurer.

SCHEDULE No. 2.

CITY OF MONTREAL CONSOLIDATED FUND.

Class C.

TERMINABLE DEBENTURES.

CITY HALL,
Montreal,   18 .

Form of certificate of shares in class C.

CERTIFICATE No.
This is to certify that
of   , at the date hereof, the registered owners, in the books of the corporation of the city of Montreal, of

AMENDMENTS TO CHARTER.

shares of one hundred dollars each, in all amounting to
dollars, of the following terminable debentures of the consolidated fund of the city of Montreal, issued under the authority of the act of the legislature of Quebec, in the Dominion of Canada, passed on the   day of   , 18   ,
(Vic., chap. ,) intituled: "An act to amend the acts relating to the corporation of the city of Montreal and for other purposes," viz : 1st issue of   payable   shares

Upon the amount of the shares in the said terminable debentures standing enregistered to the credit of the owners thereof, in the books of the corporation of the city of Montreal, the corporation of the mayor, aldermen and citizens of the said city will pay interest semi-annually, at the rate of seven per cent per annum, on the first days of May and November in each year. And the principal sum accruing at the maturity of the respective issues of the said terminable debentures will be redeemed in full, and paid to such parties as may stand enregistered proprietors in the books of the said corporation, twenty-five years after the dates of the respective issues, authorized by virtue of the act hereinbefore stated.

Sealed with the seal of the corporation of the said city of Montreal—signed by the mayor—countersigned by the city clerk, and enregistered in the books of the said corporation by the city treasurer of the said city, this   day of   , 18

(L. S.)   Mayor.
   City clerk,
Registered book   Folio
                                City Treasurer.

AMENDMENTS TO CHARTER.

SCHEDULE No. 3.

CITY OF MONTREAL CONSOLIDATED FUND.

CITY HALL,

Montreal, 18 .

Form of certificate of transfer.

This is to certify that
Montreal has this day transferred in the books of the corporation of the city of Montreal to the credit of
of
shares of one hundred dollars each, in all amounting to dollars of the consolidated fund of the city of Montreal, under the following classes, viz :

The said shares are transferable on the books of the corporation of the said city only by the said
or
attorney duly constituted,

City Treasurer.

SCHEDULE No. 4.

CITY OF MONTREAL CONSOLIDATED FUND

Form of transfer.

For value received from
of
do hereby assign and transfer unto the said
shares of one hundred dollars each, amounting to the sum of dollars, in the consolidated fund of the city of Montreal, viz :

AMENDMENTS TO CHARTER.

of Montreal water works stock (class A)   shares. of Montreal public property stock (class B)   shares. and Montreal terminable debentures (Class C)   shares.

    Witness my hand this   day of   in the year one thousand eight hundred and

Signed in presence of

Witnesses.

Signature of party transferring.

AMENDMENTS TO CHARTER.

(32 VICTORIA, CAP. 70.)

An Act to amend the Acts relating to the Corporation of the city of Montreal, and for other purposes.

[*Assented to 5th April*, 1869.]

Preamble.

WHEREAS the corporation of the city of Montreal have, by their petition, represented that it has become necessary, in the interest of the citizens of the said city, to make several alterations to its Acts of incorporation, and to introduce certain reforms and modifications in the municipal administration of the said city; Therefore, Her Majesty, by and with the advice and consent of the Legislature of Quebec, enacts as follows:

ELECTIONS.

Arrest &c of persons illegally voting.

1. Any person who, at any election of a mayor, or councillor, or councillors for the said city, or for any ward thereof, shall unlawfully attempt to vote, with the certificate of another elector, may, and shall be liable to be arrested on view by any justice of the peace for the said city of Montreal, or by any peace officer or constable, present at any such election, or by warrant of any justice of the peace, and so arrested to be committed to safe custody, or confined in the common gaol of the district of Montreal, till the close or termination of the said election, and till good and sufficient security may be taken from the parties so arrested, that they shall duly appear and

answer to any charge that may be made against them, as aforesaid; and each and every such person, on conviction of the said offence, shall forfeit and pay a fine or sum of money not exceeding one hundred dollars, current money of this province, and in default of immediate payment shall be liable to an imprisonment not exceeding three months in the common gaol or the house of correction of the said district, for each and every such offence unless such fine shall be sooner paid. *Penalty, etc.*

TAVERN LICENSES.

2. The certificate required by the eleventh section of chapter six of the consolidated statutes for Lower Canada, for obtaining a license, may be signed by twenty-five domiciled municipal electors of the ward of the said city for which such license is asked instead of fifty as heretofore. *Certificate may be signed by only 25 persons.*

3. The board of chairmen of committees established by the tenth section of the act passed in the thirty-first year of Her Majesty's reign, chapter thirty-seven, may, at the expiration of the delay fixed by the twelfth section of the last cited act, grant certificates which the parties interested may fyle, as prescribed by the eleventh section of the said act, at all times, from and after the fifteenth of March of each year, as specified in the said eleventh section; and the said board shall exercise their functions during the whole year, and, to that effect, shall sit once every month, to consider such certificates, and to confirm or reject the same at their discretion; and when any such certificate shall have been confirmed, the revenue inspector shall issue to the bearer thereof a license. *Board of chairmen to grant certificates 31 V. c. 37.*

AMENDMENTS TO CHARTER.

And may revoke the same;

4. Power and authority are also conferred upon the said board of chairmen of committees, on complaint of the police or any five proprietors of the ward in which a license may be in force, to revoke and annul the certificate upon which such license shall have been granted; and the revenue inspector, when notified to that effect by the city clerk, shall annul the said license.

And may adjudicate upon transfers of license:

5. The said board of chairmen shall have power to adjudicate upon the conveyance or transfer of a license from one person to another, or from one place to another, within the limits of the said city, and the revenue inspectors shall give effect to such decision; and the said board shall also, solely and *And may remit fines.* exclusively, exercise the right of remitting such part of any fine imposed by the recorder's court for infraction of the law on licenses as may belong to the said city.

Majority of board necessary.

6. No resolution adopted by the said board of chairmen in pursuance of the next preceding third, fourth and fifth sections, shall be valid unless the same shall have been sanctioned by the vote of the majority of the members constituting the said board.

STOCK, DEBENTURES, &C.

7. To facilitate transactions in the stock, shares and debentures of the city of Montreal consolidated fund or in any of the loans which the council of the said city are, by law, authorized to make, it is enacted that the said stock, shares or debentures may be validly transferred and made over by means of endorsement in conformity with schedule A, annexed to the present act; provided that any sum of money paid to the bearer of any such certi-

AMENDMENTS TO CHARTER. 39

ficate for interest accruing on the stock represented by such certificate shall be endorsed on the said certificate.

8. The second section of the said act thirty-first Victoria chapter thirty-seven, is hereby amended, and the interest to be paid by the said city of Montreal on the shares, stock and debentures to be issued hereafter, shall not exceed, but may be less than seven per cent, and the principal and interest of the said shares, stock and debentures may be made payable either in this province or elsewhere, and in the current money of Canada, or, in that of the place, where the said principal and interest shall be payable. Sec. 2 of 31 V c. 37 amended.

EXPROPRIATIONS.

9, The right of opposition, conferred in and by section eleven of the act passed in the twenty ninth and thirtieth Victoria, chapter fifty-six and by section nine, of the thirty-first Victoria, chapter thirty-seven, upon the majority of proprietors interested in an improvement, resolved upon by the city council of the said city, shall not apply to expropriations for improvements as laid down on the general plan of the city of Montreal, when such improvements only affect new or projected Streets, as fixed and determined upon such general plan of the city of Montreal, and not already in actual possession of the said city, when and so soon as the said plan shall be homologated and confirmed by the court according to the provisions of twenty-seventh and twenty-eighth Victoria chapter sixty; and the owners of real estate through whose property such new or projected streets are laid down shall have Sec. 11 of 29, 30 V. c. 56 and sec. 9 of 31 V. 37 not to apply in certain projected streets, after homologation of city plan.

no claim whatsoever against the said corporation for rights of servitude, accruing from the fact of such projected streets being run through their property ;

Proviso. Provided, that nothing herein contained shall be construed so as to affect the right of opposition which now exists as to the enlargement or widening of old streets, which right of opposition shall remain in full force with regard to the widening or enlargement of such old streets.

When expropriation leaves less than 30 feet, owner may compel corporation to purchase. 10. When there shall remain, after expropriation of part of any real-estate, a depth not exceeding thirty feet, the proprietor, usufructuary or administrator thereof may compel the corporation of the said city to acquire the same, for such price per foot as the commissioners of expropriation, may determine, in reference to such residue, by the said proprietor, usufructuary, or administrator giving to the said city clerk, on or before the day fixed for the commissioners to proceed to the valuation, notice of such his intention to sell and give up such residue as aforesaid.

Prothonotary to pay over to city treasurer interest on indemnities deposited.

27, 28 V. c. 60.

Proviso.

11. The prothonotary of the Superior Court shall henceforth pay and remit to the city treasurer of the said city, all interest and revenue arising from the different sums of money deposited by the said city in the hands of the said prothonotary as indemnity in virtue of the twenty-seventh and twenty-eight Victoria, chapter sixty, provided always that the poundage commission and percentage on the said sums of money shall be retained by the said prothonotary as is now provided for by law ; and all sums so deposited shall immediately after their receipt be placed by the prothonotary in a separate

AMENDMENTS TO CHARTER. 41

account at interest in one of the chartered banks doing business in the city of Montreal.

12. No person shall be capable of fulfilling the duties of commissioner of expropriation, unless such person be assessed and rated in the general assessment roll of the said city, as proprietor of one or more real estate, of the aggregate value of at least ten thousand dollars currency. Qualification of commissioners of expropriation.

13. When a special roll of assessments, or any other assessment whatsoever made by the assessors of the said city, or the commissioners of expropriation, or any municipal officer whatsoever, to defray the costs of any improvement or work executed in the public interest, shall be defective, or shall be rejected and annulled by the Superior Court, or by the Circuit Court, or the recorder's court, or by any judge of the said courts, as the case may be, it shall be the duty of the said assessors, or of the said municipal officer, or their successors in office, or of the commissioners, as the case may be, to proceed to make out a new roll of assessment or a new apportionment, in order that such improvement or work, as aforesaid, may be paid by the parties interested, when the council of the said city shall have so determined; Provided always, that this section shall not have the effect of rendering valid any such assessment roll, which may be defective by reason of the illegality of the resolutions of the council, upon which such rolls based; and provided also, that said commissioners be appointed as follows: one shall be named by the corporation, one by the parties mentioned in the roll of assessment set aside and the third by a judge of Rolls of assessment may be annulled and others ordered by Superior Court, &c.

Proviso.

Proviso; mode of appointment of commissioners.

AMENDMENTS TO CHARTER.

the Superior Court, and in case of the failure on the part either of the parties interested or of the said corporation to select an arbitrator within ten days after proper notice shall have been given to make such selection, the said arbitrator shall be appointed by a judge of the Superior Court.

RECORDER'S COURT.

Name in which certain prosecutions may be instituted.

14. And whereas doubts have been entertained as to the mode of proceeding before the recorder's court of the city of Montreal in prosecutions instituted against parties for selling spirituous, vinous or fermented liquors, without license, and as to the precise meaning of the third section of twenty-ninth Victoria, chapter fifty-eight, enacted to simplify the procedure in relation to the said prosecutions; be it enacted that prosecutions for the said offence may be instituted by and in the name of the mayor, aldermen and citizens of Montreal; and one third of all penalties in all such prosecutions shall be paid to the treasurer of the Province of Quebec.

Sec. 3 of 29 V. c. 58.

One third of penalties to go to treas. of the prov.

Imprisonment in default of fine.

15. In default of immediate payment of the fine imposed for the said offence and payable to the prosecutors, and costs thereby incurred, the defendant may be imprisoned under a warrant of commitment of the said recorder for a period of not less than two months and not exceeding six months in the common gaol of the district of Montreal, as may be deemed expedient; but the defendant may at any time obtain his liberation from such imprisonment by making full payment to the said prosecutors of the said fine and costs whether incurred before or after conviction.

AMENDMENTS TO CHARTER.

16. No keeper of a tavern, dramshop, saloon or other house or place of public entertainment in the said city, whether licensed or unlicensed, shall keep open such tavern, dramshop, saloon or other house or place of public entertainement, or shall permit tippling or drinking of intoxicating liquor therein, after the hour of ten o'clock at night and before the our of five o'clock in the morning, between the twenty-first day of March and the first day of October, and after the hour of nine o'clock at night, and before six o'clock in the morning, from the first day of October and the twenty-first day of March; and upon conviction of such offence, such keeper of tavern, dramshop, saloon, or other place of public entertainment as aforesaid, shall be liable to a penalty of not less than ten nor more than twenty dollars, and the costs of the prosecution, and, in default of immediate payment of the said fine and costs, to an imprisonment of not less than one nor more than two months, unless the said fine and costs shall be sooner paid.

Taverns, &c., to be closed between certain hours.

17. In addition to the power already accorded to the council of the city of Montreal, in and by its act of incorporation and the several acts of amendment thereof, to enforce the observance of the by-laws of the said council made under and by virtue of the acts for the purposes in the said acts expressed, it shall be lawful for the said council to impose, in and by such by-laws, a fine not exceeding twenty dollars and costs of prosecution, to be forthwith leviable on the goods and chattels of the defendant; or to enact that in default of immediate payment of the said fine and costs, the defendant may be imprisoned in the common gaol, for a period not exceeding two months, the said impri-

Additional power to enforce by-laws by fine or imprisonment or both.

44 AMENDMENTS TO CHARTER.

sonment to cease upon payment of the said fine and costs ; or to impose the said fine and costs in addition to the said imprisonment.

Punishment of persons frequenting disorderly houses.
18. All persons being found in houses of ill-fame or disorderly houses, and not giving a satisfactory account of themselves, shall be deemed loose, idle and disorderly persons, and upon conviction of the said offence, shall be condemned to pay a fine not exceeding twenty dollars and costs of prosecution, and in default of immediate payment of the fine and costs, shall be imprisoned in the common gaol, with or without hard labor, for any period not exceeding two months, unless the said fine and costs shall be sooner paid.

Preceding sections and secs. 14 & 15 of 31 V., c. 37 not to apply to criminal matters.
19. The five preceding sections, and sections fourteen and fifteen of the thirty-first Victoria, chapter thirty-seven, shall not be deemed to apply to any matter of criminal procedure before the said recorder's court.

LOANS.

Authority to effect the "Mount Royal Park Loan."
20. It shall be lawful for the corporation of the said city, to borrow a sum not exceeding three hundred and fifty thousand dollars currency to be designated as the "*Mount Royal Park Loan*,, for the purpose of acquiring and establishing a public park on and in the vicinity of the mountain of Montreal, of the extent shewn and of the form delineated in green in a certain lithographed copy drawn and made by one John Johnston, in november 1867, of a certain plan of said park, drawn by Mr. McQuisten, city surveyor, said lithographic copy being fyled in the office of the clerk of the legislative council to remain of record for all the purposes of this act, copies of which

AMENDMENTS TO CHARTER. 45

in full or on a reduced scale certified by the said clerk shall be deemed authentic for all legal purposes; and the said corporation are authorized to issue, under the signature of the mayor and the seal of the said corporation, bonds or debentures to the amount of the said sum of three hundred and fifty thousand dollars, payable twenty-five years after the date of their issue, and bearing interest at a rate not exceeding seven per cent per annum, payable on the first day of May and on the first day of November in each year, and the said bonds or debentures may be issued from time to time for such amount as may be deemed expedient, and shall, as regards the principal as well as the interest, be secured by special mortgage, by and upon the real estate acquired for the said park; and also by and upon the works to be constructed thereon; and all the extent of land described on the said plan and delineated as aforesaid and required for the purposes of the said park, shall form part of the city of Montreal, and be deemed to be within the limits of the said city for all municipal purposes, and all the powers by law vested in the corporation of the said city relating to expropriation shall apply to the said extent of land. *And to issue $350,000 of debentures for that purpose.*

Debentures to be a mortgage on the park.

21. The council of the said city are hereby authorized to levy, by means of a special assessment, to be made every year, until the paying off of the debt created for such loan, on all real estate situated within the limits of the said city, a sum sufficient to cover the interest on the said loan and the sinking fund created to pay off the same. The said council shall also have the power to sell a portion of the ground acquired for the said park as villas around the said park; but the establishment, management *Power to levy money to pay off the loan.*

Management

AMENDMENTS TO CHARTER.

of the park, and disposal of part thereof.

and supervision of the said park shall devolve upon and be left exclusively to three competent persons to be chosen and appointed by the said council, as commissioners for that purpose; provided that the quantity of land so sold for villas around said park, shall not exceed in the whole one hundred and fifty acres.

Appointment of valuating commissioners.

22. The commissioners for the valuation of the property required for the said park shall be named as follows;—one by the corporation, one by the parties whose property is to be expropriated and a third by a judge of the Superior Court, and in case of the failure either of the owner of the property to be expropriated or of the said corporation to select an arbitrator within ten days after proper notice shall have been given to make such selection, the said arbitrator shall be appointed by a judge of the Superior Court.

Park to be deemed a general improvement.

23. The said park shall be considered a general improvement interesting equally all parts of the city.

Power to borrow $500,000 for water works.

And to issue debentures therefor.

24. It shall be lawful for the corporation of the said city, to borrow a sum not exceeding five hundred thousand dollars currency, for the purpose of obtaining a larger and permanent supply of water for the said city, procuring additional storage for water, and extending the water pipe distribution in the said city; and the said corporation are authorized to issue, under the signature of the mayor and the seal of the said corporation, bonds or debentures to the amount of the said sum of five hundred thousand dollars, payable twenty-five years after the date of their issue, and bearing interest at a rate not exceeding seven per cent per annum, payable on the first

AMENDMENTS TO CHARTER. 47

day of May and the first day of November in each year; and the said bonds or debentures may be issued, from time to time, for such amount as may be deemed expedient, and shall, as regards the principal and the interest, be secured by special mortgage by and upon the real estate, works, constructions, engines, machinery and mechanism of the water works of the said city.

Debentures to be a mortgage on the works.

25. The amounts which the corporation of the said city are authorized to borrow, in virtue of the twenty-sixth and twenty-eighth sections of the present act, may be so borrowed either in this province or elsewhere, in sterling money or in the current money of this province, or in the current money of the place where made payable; and the principal and the interest may be made payable either in this province, or elsewhere, and either in the current money of Canada or in that of the place where the said principal and interest shall be made payable; and all the provisions contained in the fourth, fifth and sixth sections of the act thirty-first Victoria chapter thirty-seven, in so far only as they relate to the issue of bonds or debentures, the enregistration and transfer, the establishment of a sinking fund under the responsibility of the treasurer of the said city, and his rights and obligations in that respect shall apply also to the issuing, enregistering, transferring and paying of the bonds or debentures, the issue of which is authorized by the said twenty-sixth and twenty-eighth sections of the present act, and to the establishing of a sinking fund to pay off the said amount; provided however that, to make up the sinking fund on the aforesaid two loans, the treasurer of the said city shall be held and required to set

Said loan may be effected in the province or elsewhere.

Secs. 4, 5 & 6 of 31 V., c. 37 to apply.

Proviso.

aside and reserve, every year, two per cent, only on such part or portion of each of the said loans, as shall have been issued and negotiated, and not on the total amount of the loan, as required by the last cited act, except when such amount may have been issued in full.

MISCELLANEOUS PROVISIONS.

Sec. 10 of 23 V., c. 72, extended to certain purposes.

Junk stores.

Planting of trees.

Sale of milk.

26. Among the subjects in connection with the by-laws which the corporation of the said city are authorized by the tenth section of the act of the twenty-third year of Her Majesty's reign, chapter seventy-two, to pass, shall henceforth be included junk stores, wherein bits of brass, lead or iron, pipes, cocks, cord, old furniture, or other like articles, the plantation of trees in the streets or public squares, the sale of milk within the city limits; and the council of the said city shall have full power and authority to license and regulate all such stores as aforesaid, to compel any proprietor within the city limits to plant trees in front of his property, under the direction of the city surveyor, and upon such proprietor failing to comply with such order, to cause such plantation to be made, and to exact the cost thereof from such proprietor; to license and regulate the sale and quality of milk, to authorize its being seized and confiscated for violation of the by-laws, to provide for the inspection of milk and the manner in which the same may be disposed of after confiscation, to authorize to that effect competent officers or persons to enter into any place where milk is sold, and to stop the vehicles in which it is carried, for the purpose of having it inspected, and to adopt such other steps as may be deemed expedient in the interest

AMENDMENTS TO CHARTER. 49

and for the safety of the public, or to carry out the object in view,—the whole under such conditions and restrictions as the said council may deem advisable to impose in the public interest; and the said council may impose the penalties specified in the thirteenth section of the said act, twenty-third Victoria, chapter seventy-two for infractions of any of the said by-laws.

27. The second subsection of the tenth section of the last cited act, is hereby amended so as to confer upon the council of the said city the right to regulate by by-law the erection, use or employment of steam-boilers in the same manner as the said council is authorized to regulate the erection, use or employment of steam-engines and other machinery and establishments enumerated in the said subsection, and also to provide for the inspection and supervision of the said steam-boilers; and by such by-law, to impose the penalties mentioned in the thirteenth section of the said act, twenty-third Victoria, chapter seventy-two. *§2 of sec. 10. of 23 V. c. 72. amended as regards steam boilers.*

28. In addition to the rights, privileges and duties now devolving on and exercised by the inspector of buildings of the said city, the council of the said city may, by a by-law to be passed to that effect, authorize him to demolish any building or structure that may endanger the lives of the citizens within the limits of the said city, or to prevent or prohibit the use or occupation of said building or structure, or to do and perform such work or repair that the said inspector may deem necessary to ensure the safety of such building or structure, and to recover the cost of such work or repair from the proprietor. *Demolition or repair of dangerous buildings.*

50 AMENDMENTS TO CHARTER

Repeal of inconsistent enactments.
29. All sections of any law incompatible with the provisions of the present act, shall be, and the same are hereby repealed, but in so far only as they are inconsistent with the said provisions, and the present section shall not have the effect of reviving any act or part of an act repealed by the said law.

Certificate   Shares.

No.

CITY OF MONTREAL CONSOLIDATED FUND.

Class...............

Montreal,   18

Form of receipt for certificate.
The undersigned being at this date the   istered proprietor in the books of the corpora   of the Mayor, Aldermen and citizens of the city of Montreal, of   share   , class   of the *City of Montreal Consolidated Fund* amounting to   dollars, acknowledges to have received in lieu thereof and in full satisfaction therefor a transferable certificate for   share , class , amounting to   dollars of the said *City of Montreal Consolidated Fund* and which said transferable certificate is issued under the authority of the act of the legislature of the province of Quebec passed in the   year of Her Majesty's reign ....Vict. Cap...........

Witness

AMENDMENTS TO CHARTER.

SCHEDULE A.

Certificate.   Shares.
No.

CITY OF MONTREAL CONSOLIDATED FUND.

Class............

Montreal,   18

This certificate will entitle the bearer on presen- *Form of share certificate.*
tation and surrender hereof to be inscribed on the
Books of the Corporation of the Mayor, Aldermen
and Citizens of the city of Montreal as registered
owner of   shares, class   of the
City of Montreal Consolidated Fund amounting to
         dollars : and the interest on the same,
payable, at the rate of seven per cent *per annum* semi-annually on the first day of May and November,
will only be paid to the bearer hereof.

  City clerk   Mayor
Entered and Registered Folio
         City Treasurer.

Extracts from the Act to amend the law respecting Education in this Province.

[*Assented to* 5 *April* 1869.]

22. The annual grant to be paid for the support
of schools in the cities of Quebec and of Montreal, under the twenty-fourth, eighty-eighth, and eighty-
ninth sections of the fifteenth chapter of the Consolidated Statutes for Lower Canada, shall be in the

proportion of the populations of the said cities, and shall be apportioned by the Minister of Public Instruction, or the Superintendent of Education for the time being, between the Roman Catholic and Protestant Boards of School commissioners, according to the relative proportions of the Roman Catholic and Protestant populations in the said cities, according to the then last census.

23. The corporations of the said cities of Quebec and Montreal shall pay for the support of the schools in the said cities a sum equal to three times the amount of the share of the government grant coming to the schools of the said cities under the above provisions, and the sum coming to each of the Roman Catholic and Protestant boards of school commissioners under the following provisions shall be paid by the said corporations to the secretary-treasurers of the said boards irrespective of the collection of the tax thereinafter provided for in two equal semi-annual payments on the first of January, and on the first of July of each year, and shall be recoverable by the said boards before any court of competent civil jurisdiction with interest and costs. For the present year, the payment due on the first of July, may be delayed to the first of August.

24. The corporations of the cities of Quebec and of Montreal, shall levy annually by assessment on real estate in the said cities, a tax sufficient to cover the amount payable by them for the support of schools under the above provisions, and the said tax shall be laid, and collected and recovered at the time and in the manner provided for the other city taxes on real estate, except that if, for the present year, the time for assessing and levying the city

taxes is passed when this law shall come into force, the said tax shall be forthwith laid and levied nothwithstanding. The said tax shall be known as the " city school tax."

25. Property belonging to religious, charitable or educational institutions and corporations, and occupied by the said institutions or corporations for the objects for which they were respectively established and not held by them solely for the purpose of deriving an income therefrom shall be exempted from the said "city school tax."

26. The said "city school tax," shall be payable by the proprietors of real estate to the exclusion of the tenant, and the tenant shall not be bound to reimburse the same to the proprietor, except in the case of special agreement to that effect, and the said tax shall not be deemed to be included in any lease to be made after the passing of this act under the name of "municipal or city, or corporation taxes," or the word "all taxes," but shall be mentioned as the "city school tax." The usufructuary or the occupant, under an emphyteutic lease shall be deemed to be the proprietor for the purposes of this act, as also the occupant in case where the proprietor shall be unknown.

27. The corporation of the city of Montreal, and the assessment board in the city of Quebec, shall forthwith cause to be made, and shall hereafter cause to be made every year at the same time as the assessment, and in the same manner, a statement of the real estate, in each of the said cities. The assessors, in the said cities for the purposes of this act shall be in equal number Roman Catholics and Protestants—a Roman Catholic and a Protestant acting for each ward, and the necessary appointments for that object are hereby authorized.

28. The said statement shall bear against each lot or property the estimated value of the same, the name of the proprietor and the amount of the city school tax to be levied on the same for the year, but the latter head of information may be left out for the first year if more convenient.

29. The said statement shall be divided into four distinct panels

1. Panel number one shall consist of the real estate belonging exclusively to Roman Catholic proprietors.

2. Panel number two shall consist of the real estate belonging exclusively to protestants.

3. Panel number three shall consist of the real estate belonging to Corporations or incorporated companies and subject to taxation under this act, or to persons not belonging to the Roman Catholic or Protestant faith , or whose religious faith shall not have been ascertained, or belonging partly or jointly to persons belonging some to the Roman Catholic and others to the Protestant religion, or to persons who shall have declared in writing their desire of having their property inscribed on said panel, or to firms and commercial partnerships who shall not have declared through their agent, or one of their members, their desire of being placed on the first or on the second panel.

4. Panel number four shall consist of the real estate exempted from taxations.

AMENDMENTS TO CHARTER.

5. Properties possessed for purposes of revenue by religious, charitable or educational institutions or corporations shall be inscribed upon list number one or list number two according to the religious denomination to which such institutions or corporations shall belong or in accordance with the declarations made by each of them to that effect, and if the religious denomination is not apparent and if no such declaration has been made they shall be placed upon list number three.

30. The said statement so soon as completed shall be placed in the office of the city treasurer, and notice thereof shall forthwith be given in at least two newspapers published in the french language, and two published in the english language in the said cities, and during thirty days after the publication of the first of the said notices, the said panels shall be opened for inspection.

31. During the thirty days it shall be lawful for either board of school commissioners or for any person or corporation whose name shall have been entered wrongly or omitted on any of the said panels, or who shall find that the name of any other person or corporation has been entered wrongly or omitted in any of the said panels, to file any complaint they may have to make with the city treasurer, who shall accordingly alter and revise the said panels if necessary, and within three days it shall be lawful to appeal from his decision to the Recorder.

32. After the expiring of the said delays, the said panels shall be acted upon for the purposes of this act for the then current year, but may be further corrected as hereinafter provided. And all accounts

56 AMENDMENTS TO CHARTER.

for the said tax sent and delivered to the rate payers and the receipts given to the same shall bear conspicuously on their face the words "panel number one, Roman Catholic school tax," "panel number two, Protestant school tax," or "panel number three, neutral school tax" as the case may be according to the panel on which the property shall have been inscribed. It shall be lawful for each board of school commissioners or for any person or corporation after the expiration of the said thirty days, but at least thirty days before the second payment to be made by the corporation after the making of the said panels, to bring any complaints they may have in relation to the said panels before the treasurer after giving three days notice thereof to the board of school commissioners, whose share of the sum may be diminished by reason of such complaints, with a right of appeal within three days to the Recorder, and according to the decision of the treasurer or the recorder, the panel or panels shall be amended, and on the forthcoming payments the error shall be rectified for both payments.

After the second payment it shall be lawful for the corporation, if they see fit to declare by resolution that the statement and panels as amended shall be in force for three years from the date of the said panels, and in such case no other statement and panels shall be made until such statement and panels are in force.

33. The sum to be paid by the corporations semi-annually for the support of the schools shall be apportioned as follows:

1. A sum proportionate to the value of the pro-

AMENDMENTS TO CHARTER.

perty inscribed on panel number three shall be divided between the Roman Catholic and Protestant Boards in the relative ratio of the Roman Catholic and Protestant populations in the said cities according to the then last census.

2. The remainder of the said amount shall be divided between the Roman Catholic and Protestant Boards in the relative ratio of the value of the property inscribed on panel number one and on panel number two respectively.

35. The school commissioners of the said cities, during the next twenty years, shall have the power of laying aside annually a portion of their revenues not exceeding one fourth for the purchase of lots and for the construction of school houses, without any limitation as to the amount to be spent on each school house, any law to the contrary notwithstanding, And it shall be lawful for the said boards with the approval of the Lieutenant-Governor in Council to raise loans for the said purposes, and to transfer as security for such loans a part of their annual claims on the corporation for the following years subject to the above limitation, and the said board may with the approbation aforesaid raise money in advance for the said purpose by issuing debentures of not less than $100,00 each redeemable in not more than twenty years and for an amount not exceeding in the whole for any one of the said boards the sum of $100,000, and in such case the portion of their revenue set aside annually as aforesaid or so much thereof as they may determine shall be applied to the forming of a sinking fund for the redemption of such debentures.

AMENDMENTS TO CHARTER.

Extracts from the Act to amend the law respecting Jurors and Juries.

[*Assented to* 5 *April* 1869.

QUALIFICATION OF GRAND AND PETIT JURORS.

2. The following persons, (subject to the exemptions and disqualifications hereinafter provided for), are qualified to act, and shall, when duly chosen and summoned, be bound to serve as grand jurors, namely :

2. Every male person resident in a town or city containing at least twenty thousand inhabitants, or in the *banlieue* thereof, who is assessed upon the valuation roll of such town or city, as proprietor of immovable property of an assessed total value above two thousand dollars, or as occupant or lessee of immovable property of an assessed annual value above three hundred dollars ; or who is a justice of the peace and has duly qualified as such :

3. Every male person resident within the limits of any other municipality, any part whereof is situate within ten leagues of the place of holding the court, in the district in which he resides, who is assessed upon the valuation roll of such municipality as proprietor of immovable property of an assessed total value above one thousand five hundred dollars, or as occupant or lessee of immovable property of an assessed annual value above one hundred and fifty dollars.

3. The following persons, (subject to the exemptions and disqualifications hereinafter provided for,) are qualified to act, and shall, When duly chosen and summoned, be bound to serve as petit jurors:

2. Every male person resident in a town or city containing at least twenty thousand inhabitants, or in the *banliene* thereof, who is assessed upon the valuation-roll of such town or city, as proprietor of immovable property of an assessed total value of at least eight hundred dollars, but not more than two thousand dollars, or as occupant or lessee of immovable property of an assessed annual value of at least one hundred dollars, but not more than three hundred dollars, except justices of the peace duly qualified as such:

3. Every male person resident within the limits of any other municipality, whereof any part is situate within ten leagues of the place of holding the court in the district in which he resides, who is assessed upon the valuation roll of such municipality, as proprietor of immovable property of an assessed total value of at least six hundred dollars, but not more than one thousand five hundred dollars, or as occupant or lessee of immovable property of an assessed annual value of at least eighty dollars, but not more than one hundred and fifty dollars.

DISQUALIFICATIONS.

4. The following persons are disqualified from serving as grand or petit jurors respectively :

1. Persons who are not qualified as such under the foregoing provisions of this act;

2. Persons below the age of 21 years;

3. Persons afflicted with blindness, deafness, or

any other physical infirmity incompatible with the discharge of the duties of a juror;

4. Persons who are arrested or under bail upon a charge of treason or felony, or who have been convicted thereof;

5. Aliens, except in cases where, according to law, one half of the jury must be composed of aliens.

EXEMPTIONS.

5. The following persons are exempt from serving as jurors:

1. Members of the clergy;

2. Members of the privy council, or of the senate or of the house of commons of Canada, or persons in the employ of the government of Canada;

3. Members of the executive council, legislative council or legislative assembly of Quebec, or persons in the employ of the government of Quebec or of the Legislature thereof;

4. Practising advocates and attorneys;

5. Prothonotaries, clerks of the crown, clerks of the peace, and clerks of the circuit court; the clerk, treasurer and other municipal officers of the cities of Quebec and Montreal;

6. Sheriffs and coroners;

7. Officers of Her Majesty's courts;

8. Gaolers and keepers of houses of correction;

9. Officers of the army and navy on full pay;

10. Pilots duly licensed;

11. School-masters not exercising any other profession;

AMENDMENTS TO CHARTER.

12. All persons employed in the running of railway trains;

13. Physicians, surgeons and apothecaries, practising their professions;

14. Cashiers, tellers, clerks, and accountants of incorporated banks;

15. Masters and crews of steamboats, during the season of navigation;

16. All persons employed in the working of grist mills;

17. Officers, non-commissioned officers and privates of the active militia;

18. Firemen;

19. Registrars;

20. Persons above sixty years of age;

21. The persons mentioned in section twenty-three of the act fourth and fifth Victoria, chapter ninety.

JURY LISTS.

6. Within three months after this act comes into force, the clerk or secretary-treasurer of every local municipality, being wholly or in part within thirty miles of the place of holding the court in the district in which such municipality is situate, shall cause to be delivered, without charge, to the sheriff of such district, an extract from the assessment or valuation roll then in force in such municipality, giving the names of all persons named on such roll, who reside within the municipality and are qualified to act respectively as grand jurors and petit jurors.

AMENDMENTS TO CHARTER.

7. Within two months after the completion of every new valuation or assessment roll in such municipality, the clerk or secretary-treasurer shall in like manner cause to be delivered, without charge, to the said sheriff, a similar extract from such roll, giving the names of all persons named thereon, who reside within the municipality and are qualified to act respectively as grand jurors and petit jurors.

8. Before delivering to the sheriff the extract mentioned in the two preceding sections, the clerk or secretary-treasurer, after having given at least eight days' public notice thereof, shall submit the said extract to the council of the municipality, at a special meeting, convened for such purpose. The council shall, at such meeting, examine the said extract, make such corrections therein as it deems necessary, and approve the same, and in testimony of such approval, the head of the council, or the councilor presiding at such meeting, and also the clerk or secretary-treasurer shall sign the said extract.

9. In the interval between the completion of each such valuation roll and the completion of the next, the said clerk or secretary-treasurer shall also, every twelve months, deliver to the sheriff, free of charge, a supplement, containing the names of all persons who, to his knowledge, since the delivery of the previous extract or supplement have died, or no longer reside within the limits of the municipality, or have become disqualified or exempt from serving as jurors, or have been discovered to have been erroneously included in or omitted from the previous extract or supplement, and such clerk or secretary-

treasurer shall in each case give, with the said extract or supplement, all necessary details and information for identifying each person named therein.

10. The said clerk or secretary-treasurer shall ascertain, by enquiries and all other necessary means, what persons within his municipality are disqualified or exempt from serving as jurors, and he shall not knowingly include in any extract or supplement, to be furnished to the sheriff under this act, the name of any person so disqualified or exempt under sections four and five of this act.

11. The said clerk or secretary-treasurer shall make and keep among the records of his office, and open gratuitously to public inspection, a duplicate of every extract or supplement furnished to the sheriff under this act.

12. Every such extract and every such supplement shall be accompanied with an affidavit of the clerk or secretary-treasurer, taken before a justice of the peace, and swearing to his belief in the correctness of the said extract or supplement, and of the information furnished therewith.

13. Every such extract and supplement shall state the christian name or names of the persons named therein, their occupation and residence, whether they are assessed as proprietors, or as occupants, or lessees, or otherwise, and the amount of such assessment; and for the purposes of this section, as well as for all purposes of this act, the clerk or secretary-treasurer shall be deemed to be an officer of the court.

23. If any clerk or secretary-treasurer of any municipality fails to cause any extract or supplement, as the case may be, to be transmitted to the sheriff, within the time and in the manner prescribed by this act, the sheriff shall procure the same from the secretary-treasurer ; and he may recover from the municipality his disbursements in and about procuring the same, including all travelling expenses of a messenger, if one be sent ; together with a sum equal to the amount so disbursed, by way of penalty for such failure, with costs, by suit in his own name, before any competent tribunal.

47. Every clerk or secretary-treasurer of any municipality who shall, within six days, neglect to transmit to the sheriff any extract or supplement required of him under this act, shall incur a penalty of twenty dollars, and a further penalty of five dollars for every day, subsequent to the service upon him of any information or complaint for such neglect, during which he shall continue to be in default.

(31, VICTORIA, CAP. 32.)

An act to provide for the appointment of a Fire Marshal for the cities of Montreal and Quebec and to define his powers and duties.

[Assented to, 24th February, 1868.]

WHEREAS the destruction of property by fire in the cities of Montreal and Quebec frequently occurs under circumstances giving rise to strong suspicion that such fires were not accidental, and it is expedient to provide more effectual means of enquiry into the cause and origin of every fire occurring in the said cities, and of securing the prompt arrest of persons suspected of incendiarism; *Preamble.*

Her Majesty, by and with the advice and consent of the Legislature of Quebec, enacts as follows :

1. There shall be in each of the cities of Montreal and Quebec, an officer to be known and designated as the fire marshal of Montreal and Quebec as the case may be. *Fire marshals for Quebec and Montreal.*

2. The lieutenant-governor in council shall appoint from time to time a fit and proper person to fill the office of fire marshal in each of the cities of Montreal and Quebec. *To be named by lieut.-governor.*

3. Whenever any fire has occurred in such cities, whereby any house or other building; or any property whatever therein, has been or is exposed to be wholly or in part consumed or injured by such fire, *His duties.*

AMENDMENTS TO CHARTER.

it shall be the duty of the fire marshall to institute an enquiry into the cause or origin of such fire, and whether it was kindled by design or was the result of negligence or accident, and in so far as the same is practicable, either in person or by some competent person employed by him for that purpose.

His powers.

4. The fire marshal shall *ex officio* possess all the power, authority and jurisdiction of any judge of sessions, recorder or coroner for all purposes connected with the said enquiry, and shall have power to summon before him all persons whom he deems capable of giving information or evidence touching or concerning such fire.

He may examine on oath.

5. Such persons shall be examined under oath before the fire marshal, who is hereby authorised to administer such oath, and he shall reduce their examinations to writing.

May issue warrants if party fails to attend on summons.

6. If any person summoned to appear before the fire marshal, neglects or refuses to appear at the time and place specified in the summons, then on proof of the service of such summons either personally or by leaving the same for him at his last or most usual place of abode, the fire marshal may issue a warrant under his hand and seal to bring and to have such person at a time and place to be therein mentioned.

Or if it is probable he will not attend.

7. If the fire marshal be satisfied by evidence upon oath or affirmation, that it is probable that such person will not attend to give evidence without being compelled so to do, then instead of issuing a summons he may issue his warrant in the first instance.

Imprisonment for refusing to be

8. If on the appearance of a person so summoned before the fire marshal either in obedience to such

AMENDMENTS TO CHARTER.

summons or being brought before him by virtue of a warrant, such person refuses to be examined upon oath or affirmation concerning the premises, or refuses to take such oath or affirmation, or having taken such oath or affirmation, refuses to answer the questions concerning the premises then put to him, without giving any just excuse for such refusal, the fire marshal may, by warrant under his hand and seal, commit the person so refusing to the common gaol of the district, there to remain and be imprisonned for any time not exceeding ten days, unless in the mean time he consents to be examined and to answer concerning the premises. *Sworn or to answer.*

9. The fire marshal shall have power to arrest or cause to be arrested any person or persons suspected of having set fire to any house, building or property, either before or pending the inquiry, and should the evidence adduced before him be such as to afford reasonable grounds for believing that the fire was not accidental, and was kindled by design, he shall issue his warrant for the arrest of the offender or persons suspected, if known and not already in custody, and proceed with the examination and the committal of the accused for trial in the manner provided by chapter one hundred and two of the consolidated statutes of Canada. *Arrest of persons suspected of having set fire. C. S. C. c. 102.*

10. Any summons or warrant to secure the attendance of witnesses, or warrant of arrest, may be served or executed within the district of Montreal, and in any other district in the province of Quebec, or county or place in the province of Ontario: provided always, that where a warrant is to be executed out of the district of Montreal, or in the province of Ontario, the same shall be backed by any justice of *How summons and warrant may be executed out of the district.*

the peace within whose jurisdiction the same is to be executed, in the manner provided by chapter one hundred and two of the consolidated statutes of Canada.

Marshal to have certain powers of a judge of sessions or recorder.
11. The fire marshal shall have all the authority and jurisdiction of a judge of sessions or recorder for the arrest of all persons disturbing the peace at any such fire, or suspected of stealing any property whatever, at such fire, and to cause the offenders or persons so suspected to be brought before the judge of sessions, recorder or any justice of the peace to be dealt with according to law.

He may command services of police.
12. The fire marshal shall be entitled to command the services of one or more police officers or police- of the said city during such enquiries, and for the service of any summons or execution of warrants is- issued by him.

He shall deposit his proceedings with the clerk of the peace.
13. It shall be the duty of the fire marshal to return all depositions, examinations and proceedings had before him to the clerk of the peace for the districts of Montreal and Quebec, within eight days after the close of each enquiry.

His remuneration.
14. The fire marshal shall be entitled to receive for every original subpœna twenty cents, and for each copy five cents, and for every warrant, warrant of arrest, or warrant of commitment fifty cents, and for his services pending each enquiry, ten dollars for the first day, and five dollars per day for each subsequent day, and in the event of its being advisable to protract the enquiry, from the absence of witnesses or any other cause, beyond the seventh day of the enquiry, the total remuneration to be paid to him shall not exceed forty dollars.

AMENDMENTS TO CHARTER.

15. The cost of each enquiry shall be paid by the insurance company or companies, having insured the property or any one of the buildings, destroyed or injured by the fire, and in no case shall the corporation of the city be liable to pay the expense of any enquiry if the building be not insured, provided the contents of the same are; and if neither are insured, then the city treasurer shall be bound to pay the fire marshal the sum of ten dollars and no more, for the enquiry, in addition to the costs of the summonses and warrants issued, and the city treasurer shall be bound to pay the same on production of the certificate of the chief engineer of the fire department that such enquiry has been held within five days of the occurrence of such fire; and in like manner, the insurance company or companies shall be bound to pay *pro rata* according to the amount of each policy, the expense of said enquiries, on a like certificate and upon refusal to pay within three days of the delivery of such certificate, the amount may be recovered before the judge of sessions, recorder or a justice of the peace, summarily upon complaint of the fire marshal with costs.

<small>Costs of investigations to be paid by insurance companies or by corporations, according to circumstances.</small>

16. The provisions of chapter eighty-eight of the consolidated statutes of Canada, in so far as they relate to the cities of Montreal and Quebec and such portion of any acts of parliament as confers upon the councils of the said cities power to enact by-laws authorizing such enquiries, are hereby repealed.

<small>C. S.C. c. 88. &c., repealed</small>

32 VICTORIA, CAP. 29.

An Act to amend the Act 31 Victoria, Chapter 32, respecting the Fire Marshals for the Cities of Montreal and Quebec, and to change their name of office to that of Fire Commissioner.

[Assented to 5th April, 1869.]

HER MAJESTY, by and with the advice and consent of the Legislature of Quebec, enacts as follows :

31 V. c. 32 ss 14 & 15 repealed.

1. The fourteenth and fifteenth sections of the act thirty-first Victoria, chapter thirty-two, in so far as the same relate to the city of Montreal, are hereby repealed, and the following provisions substituted :

Corporation of Montreal to pay Fire marshals of that city.

14. The fire marshal for the city of Montreal, appointed under the said acts, shall, from and after the first day of May next, be entitled to an annual salary of sixteen hundred dollars to be divided equally between the incumbents of the said office, so long as the said office is held by more than one person, to be paid by the corporation of Montreal, in quarterly payments ; and in addition to the said salary the said fire marshal shall be entitled to receive from the said corporation for every original subpœna twenty cents, and for each copy thereof, five cents, and for every warrant, warrant of arrest, or warrant of commitment, fifty cents.

15. The said corporation shall be entitled to recover from the Fire Insurance Companies, doing business in the said city, two thirds of the amount so paid by it, in such manner and at such periods as may be determined by by-law to be made for that purpose, and which by-law it is hereby respectively authorized to make, and from time to time to change or alter; and by such by-law the said corporation may establish the proportion to be paid by each of the said Fire Insurance Companies. *Corporation may recover two thirds of amount from insurance companies.*

2. The fire marshals for the cities of Quebec and Montreal shall hereafter be called Fire Commissioners, and the words " Fire Commissioner" are hereby substituted for the words " Fire Marshall" wherever the same occur in the said act. *Fire Marshals to be called " Fire Commissioners."*

Extract from an Act for establishing a general system of Police in this Province" (33 Vic, cap 24)

Assented to 1st *February* 1870

51. Every city or municipality in which a police force is or shall hereafter be maintained, otherwise than under the provisions of this act, shall be bound whenever required so to do by the Lieutenant-Governor in Council, to place a certain number, not exceeding thirty of the men of such force, under the control of the sheriff of the District, during each term of the Court of Queen's Bench holding criminal pleas, and each term of general or quarter sessions of the peace, and during eight days before, and eight days after each such term.

52. It shall be the duty of such men :

1. To attend upon the court and to execute all warrants and perform all duties and services in relation thereto which may lawfully be performed by constables.

2. To perform all duties which may be lawfully performed by constables in relation to the escort and conveyance of convicts and other prisoners, or lunatics, to or from gaols, courts, lunatic asylums and other places.

53. If such city or municipality should refuse or neglect to comply with the above provisions of section fifty-one, the sheriff may employ and pay such other men as may be required, and recover the amount of

any expenses so incurred by him from such city or municipality, by action before any court of competent jurisdiction, and in default of payment within fifteen days after the judgment rendered in his favor in any such action he may proceed to levy the same in accordance with the provisions of section thirty-five.

Extract from An Act further to amend the law respecting Education in this Province"(33 Vic, cap 25.)

Assented to 1st *February* 1870.

1. Whenever the school commissioners of either of the cities of Quebec or Montreal, shall have determined to lay aside any portion of their revenues for the purchase of land or the construction of one or more school-houses, and shall have obtained the approval of the lieutenant-governor in council for the purpose, as provided in section thirty-five of the statutes of the province of Quebec, thirty-second Victoria, chapter sixteen, the said school commissioners shall notify the city treasurer thereof, and of the amount so determined to be set aside, and may thereupon issue their bonds for such loan, in such sums payable at such times, and bearing such rate of interest as to them shall seem advisable, and to the extent that such loan is authorised.

2. It shall be the duty of the city treasurer, on the presentation to him of the said bonds, to acknowledge signification thereof, and he shall thereafter, from year to year, retain, on behalf of the corporation sufficient of the revenues levied for shool purposes,

which would become payable to such school commissioners, to create a sinking fund for the redemption of the said bonds when they mature, out of which the holders shall be entitled to be paid by the corporation.

3. On the amounts so retained the city treasurer shall allow the said school commissioners interest at six per cent per annum, which shall be capitalized annually, for the time the funds shall remain in the custody of the corporation, and shall pay the revenues or accounts so retained, with the accrued interest thereon, in redemption of the bonds as they fall due, accounting to the school commissioners for any remaining surplus or requiring of them payment in case of deficiency.

4. The signature of the city treasurer, acknowledging signification of the bonds respectively, shall be evidence in favor of the holders thereof, that such bonds have been duly authorized, and will be provided for by such sinking fund.

5. Any agreement not conforming to the foregoing provisions, may be made between the corporation and the shool commissioners to regulate the said sinking fund, and the manner in which it may be made up and retained by the corporation; but, if no such agreement is made, the said provisions shall apply; and, in any case, the signature of the city treasurer acknowledging signification of the bonds respectively, shall be evidence in favor of the holders thereof, that such bonds have been duly authorised, and will be provided for out of the sinking fund.

(33 VICTORIA, CAP. 27)

Assented to 1st February 1870

An Act to repeal section 16 of 32 Victoria chap. 70, relating to the closing of taverns, dramshops, saloons or other houses or places of public entertainment, and to substitute other provisions therefor.

HER MAJESTY, by and with the advice and consent of the legislature of Quebec, enacts as follows:

1. Section sixteen of the act of this province, thirty-second Victoria, chapter seventy, is hereby repealed, and the following provisions are substituted therefor:

1. The council of the said city of Montreal shall forthwith and within the period of one month from the passing of this act regulate by by-law the hours for opening, and closing all inns, taverns, public billiard rooms, saloons, dram-shops, hotels and other houses or places of public entertainment, and in the discretion of the said council determine by such by-law what shall be the hours of opening and closing said establishments respectively; and further prohibit by such by-law the keepers of such establishments from permitting tippling or drinking of spirituous or fermented liquors and all persons from

tippling or drinking therein during the hours prohibited by such by-law, and such by-law shall forthwith be transmitted to the lieutenant-governor in council for approval, and such approval shall be attested by notice published in the *Quebec Official Gazette.*

2. All persons offending against such by-law shall be liable to a penalty of not less than ten dollars nor more than twenty dollars, and the costs of the prosecution, and in default of immediate payment of the said fine and costs to an imprisonment of not less than one, nor more than two months, unless the said fine and costs shall be sooner paid.

3. It shall not be lawful for any person having no license to sell spirituous, vinous or fermented liquors, to keep or suffer to be kept on his premises or possessions, or under his charge, for the purposes of sale by retail, any ale, wine, rum or any spirituous or fermented liquor, or any mixed liquor, a part of which is ale, wine, rum or any spirituous or fermented liquors.

4. It shall be the duty of every policeman to enter all unlicensed taverns, saloons, dram-shops, houses or places of public entertainment and other like places of common resort, wherein it is suspected that spirituous, vinous or fermented liquors, are kept for sale by retail, and to search for the same, and upon discovery thereof to seize and remove the said spirituous, vinous or fermented liquors, and the vessels containing the same.

5. The possession of said spirituous, vinous or fermented liquors, in such places of common resort, shall be deemed sufficient evidence of its having been kept for sale by retail, without further proof.

6. Persons offending against the provisions of paragraph two, of section first of this act, shall, in addition to the penalty herein after imposed, incur the forfeiture of the liquor and vessels containing the same which, by the conviction, shall be declared forfeited, and said liquors ordered to be destroyed; and on the second or any subsequent conviction for the said offence, the offender, in addition to the forfeiture, but in lieu of the penalty, shall be committed to the common gaol of the district for the space of three calendar months.

PART SECOND.

BYLAWS

OF

THE CITY OF MONTREAL

PASSED

SINCE THE LAST CODIFICATION

IN

1865.

By-
it
o1
w:

Wn
prevei
and o1
and by
cap. 72
may, b
count
within

BY-LAWS.

No. 1.

By-law to amend By-law chapter thirty concerning Sidewalks.

[*Passed 23rd January* 1866.]

(Annulled—see By-law No. 47.)

No. 2.

By-law to allow a discount on water rates in certain cases, and to charge interest on arrears of assessments, taxes and water rates.

[*Passed 16th April* 1866.]

Preamble. WHEREAS it is expedient to adopt measures to prevent the accumulation of arrears of Assessments and other City dues, and whereas it is provided in and by the sixteenth Section of the Act 23rd Vic., cap. 72, that the Council of the said City of Montreal, may, by a By-law, allow such rate or rates of discount on Assessments, Taxes, and Water Rates, paid within a certain delay, and charge such interest on arrears of assessments, taxes and Water rates, as the said Council may consider expedient :—

It is ordained and enacted by the said Council, and the said Council do hereby ordain and enact as follows :

Sec. 1. (Repeals Sec. 18, of By-law, Chapter five.)

Discount on water rates.
Sec. 2. A discount of five per cent shall be allowed to all persons supplied with water from the Montreal Water Works, who shall pay the water rates imposed on them in and by the said By-law, chapter five, on or before the Fifteenth day of August in each year.

On assessments, etc.
Sec. 3. On all arrears of assessments, taxes or water rates, in the said City of Montreal, which shall remain due and unpaid, on the First day of May next, there shall be charged interest at the rate of six per cent per annum, from the said First day of May next until final payment.

Ibid.
Sec. 4. On all assessments, taxes or water rates in the said City of Montreal, which shall remain due and unpaid on the First day of November next, and on the First day of November in each and every subsequent year, there shall be charged interest at the rate of six per cent, per annum, from the said First day of November, until final payment.

No. 3.

By-law to levy a special assessment on Real Estate in Notre-Dame street.

[Passed 4th July 1866.]

WHEREAS the Council of the City of Montreal, on Preamble. the Sixth day of July, one thousand eight hundred and sixty-four, resolved to acquire certain pieces or parcels of ground in Notre-Dame Street, for the purpose of widening the said Street, in accordance with the Thirtieth Section of the Act 27 and 28 Vic., cap. 60, and have in fact acquired, in pursuance of the provisions of the said Act, all the pieces or parcels of ground required for the widening of the second Section of the said street, the aggregate cost of which amounts to the sum of Fifty-three Thousand One Hundred and Twenty-one Dollars and Sixty-one Cents, as appears by the Report of the Commissioners for Notre-Dame Street, which was duly confirmed and homologated on the Seventh day of February, one thousand eight hundred and sixty-five, and by the deposits made in the hands of the Prothonotary of the Superior Court in and for the District of Montreal for the said Second Section of Notre-Dame Street ;—And whereas it is provided by the fourth sub-section of section thirty of the said Act, that one-half of the cost of the said improvement shall be borne by the said Corporation, and the other half by the Proprietors in the said Notre-Dame Street, by means of a Special Assessment to be levied upon the real estate fronting on Notre-

Dame Street, the whole of which shall be equally rated or assessed to provide one-half the expense of the said improvement, and that the assessed value of all real estate fronting on the said street for the year one thousand eight hundred and sixty-four shall be held to be the assessed value thereof for all the purposes of the said improvement :—And whereas it is also provided by the thirty-first Section of the said Act, that the said Council may, after the homologation of the Report of the said Commissioners for each Section of the said street, levy, by By-law, a special rate or assessment, as aforesaid, sufficient to cover one-half of the expenditure incurred in the widening of each section of the said street ;—And whereas it is now incumbent upon the said Council to levy, by Special Assessment, under the provisions aforesaid, on all real estate fronting on Notre-Dame Street, one half of the said sum of *Fifty-three Thousand One Hundred and Twenty-one Dollars and sixty-one Cents* to wit : the sum of *Twenty-six Thousand Five Hundred and sixty Dollars and Eighty Cents ;*

It is ordained and enacted by the said Council, and the said Council do hereby ordain and enact ;

Rate of assessment.

That a special Assessment at the rate of *one dollar and nineteen cents* for every *one hundred dollars* of the assessed value of all real estate fronting on Notre-Dame street, the said assessed value as set forth and established in and by the Assessment books for the year one thousand eight hundred and sixty-four, be made and levied upon the proprietors of real estate, fronting on Notre-Dame street aforesaid ; which said special assessment shall be due and payable on the tenth day of July instant, and applied towards the payment of the sum of *twenty six thousand five hundred and sixty dollars and eighty cents*, being one half of the cost of widening the Second Section of Notre-Dame street as aforesaid.

No. 4.

By-law to open a new street, and to discontinue part of another street in the St. Antoine ward of the said city.

[*Passed 11th September 1866.*]

WHEREAS, it is deemed expedient, in the interest of the Public, to open a new street from Chaboillez Square to Mountain Street, and to discontinue a portion of St. Felix Street; *Preamble.*

It is ordained and enacted by the said Council, and the said Council do hereby ordain and enact:

That a street, to be called "Albert" Street, be opened from Chaboillez Square to Mountain Street, at a width of eighty feet, English measure; and that that section of St. Felix Street, tinted red on the plan hereunto annexed, extending from the line of the said Albert Street towards St. Bonaventure Street, and measuring one hundred and seventy-one feet six inches on the south-west line of St. Felix Street, and one hundred and seventy-six feet on the north-east line thereof, be henceforth discontinued. *Albert street opened and part of St. Felix street discontinued.*

No. 5.

By-law to prevent Carters from transporting Dead bodies in covered Carriages.

[*Passed* 11*th September* 1866.]

Repealed.—See By-law No. 50, Sec. 36.

No. 6.

By-law to amend By-law, chapter eleven to establish and regulate the City passenger Railway.

[*Passed* 17*th October* 1866.]

Preamble.

SEC. 1. Whereas the Montreal City Passenger Railway Company have, by their Petition submitted to the said Council, under date of thirteenth December last past, represented that the conditions imposed upon them by the By-Law of this Council, chapter XI, and described under number Two Hundred and Sixty-five (265) in the Act of Incorporation of the said Company, 24 Victoria, chapter 84, are so onerous that they can no longer run their road with profit; and whereas this Council deem it advantageous, in the public interest, to partly comply with the said Petition,—the following changes and modifications are hereby made to the said By-Law, chapter XI.

Sec. 2.—It shall be optional with the said Company to lay or not to lay the rails of their track in any of the streets mentioned in the first section of the said By-Law, chapter XI., in which their road is not already built; provided, however, that they shall be held to complete any section of such unfinished road on receiving from the Corporation twelve months, previous notice to that effect; and such notice once given, the said Company, failing to comply therewith, shall forfeit their right or privilege to build such section of their road. *Company may or may not lay rails, etc.*

Sec. 3.—The said Company shall have the right to lay their track in Ste. Catherine Street from Mountain Street to Guy Street, and in Guy Street, from Ste. Catherine Street to Sherbrooke Street, whenever they may deem it expedient so to do; and these new tracks shall form part of the Second District. *Track in Ste. Catherine-st.*

Sec. 4.—The Seventh Section of the said By-law, chapter XI., is hereby amended as follows:—The Company shall be held to keep the Roadway between their rails, and twelve inches on each side thereof, paved, macadamized or gravelled, as the case may be, so as to suit the kind of paving used in the Streets through which their lines run. *Roadway between the rails.*

Sec. 5.—Every day from *Seven* o'clock A. M. to *Nine* o'clock P. M., a car shall run (when cars are employed) through the first District, at intervals of *fifteen* minutes, and through the other Districts at intervals of *twenty* minutes; but when the track is encumbered with snow or ice in the fall of the year, the Company shall not be held strictly to the foregoing hours. *Cars—when to run.*

Sleighs. SEC. 6.—In winter, with the exception of the First District, the Company may run their sleighs at such hours and in such of the streets in which their rails are laid, as in their opinion may best serve the public wants; the City Council, however, reserve to themselves, at any time hereafter, the privilege to fix the hours at which the said Company shall be held to run their sleighs.

Fare. SEC. 7.—The Company shall be entitled to charge any rate not exceeding *Five Cents*, for the conveyance of a passenger from one point to another on any one District of their road; and the Twenty-fourth Section of the said By-law, chapter XI., is amended accordingly.

Repeal of former provisions. SEC. 8.—Such provisions only of the said By-law, chapter XI., as are repugnant to the present By-law are hereby repealed.

Penalty. SEC. 9.—The penalty provided in the Twenty-ninth Section of the said By-law, chapter XI., for any infringement of the obligations imposed on the said Company, shall equally apply to the conditions imposed on the said Company by the present By-law.

No. 7.

By-law to remove the Hay Market from Victoria Square to the old College garden on College Street.

[*Passed 16th November 1866.*]

Preamble WHEREAS it has been deemed expedient to remove the Hay Market and Weigh-House from Victoria Square to the lot of ground recently acquired by the Corporation of this City from the Gentlemen of the Seminary of St. Sulpice, and commonly known as "The College Garden."

It is ordained and enacted by the said Council, and the said Council do hereby ordain and enact as follows :—

Sec. 1. The Hay Market and Weigh House, established on Victoria Square, in this city, shall be changed and removed to the lot of ground, so as aforesaid purchased from the Gentlemen of the Seminary of Montreal, and which is bounded by College, Inspector, William and George Streets. *Victoria Square Hay Market discontinued.*

Sec. 2. The said lot of ground in the preceding Section described, shall be, and the same is hereby constituted and established, the Hay Market, Number One, of this City, in lieu and place of the Hay Market heretofore existing and established on Victoria Square, which said latter Hay Market is hereby, and from henceforth abolished; and the Weigh House and scales recently erected on the above described lot of ground, shall be the Weigh House and Scales to be hereafter and henceforth used and employed in weighing hay and straw, in lieu and place of the Weigh House and Scales on Victoria Square, heretofore used for that purpose. *Hay Market established on College Ground.*

Sec. 3. All the provisons of By-law, Chap. XIX, (of the Consolided By-laws) which relate to, govern, or in any wey concern the said Hay Market on Victoria Square, or the Weigh house and scales thereon, or the Clerk thereof (who is hereby constituted and appointed the Clerk of the new Hay Market and Weigh House hereby established

2

on the above described lot of ground,) shall extend and apply to the said Hay Market, to the said Weigh House and Scales thereon and to the said Clerk thereof; and shall be in as full force and operation, and have as much effect on the said new Hay Market and in relation to the said Weigh House and Scales thereon and with the Clerk thereof, as if the said provisions had been enacted expressly for and in relation to the said new Hay Market and the said Weigh House and Scales thereon, and the said Clerk thereon; and all and every the duties, rates and taxes heretofore imposed levied and collected on the said Hay Market on Victoria Square, under and by virtue of the said By-law, Chapter XIX., shall from henceforth be imposed, levied and collected on the said new Hay Market hereby established, in the said Weigh House thereon and by the said Clerk thereof, in the like form and manner that the same heretofore have been and yet are imposed, levied and collected on the said Weigh House thereon and by the said Clerk thereof.

No. 8.

By-law to impose a duty on Billiard Tables.

[*Passed 4th February* 1867.]

Repealed—see By-law No. 20.

No. 9.

By-law to define the duties and attributions of the Auditor for the City of Montreal.

[*Passed 4th May* 1867.]

Repealed, see By-law No. 21.

No. 10.

By-law of the Council of the City of Montreal, to levy a Special Assessment on real estate in Notre Dame Street.

[*Passed 8th May* 1867.]

Special assessment.

Preamble :—A special Assessment at the rate of *two dollars fifty-two cents and three quarters of a cent* for every *one hundred dollars* of the assessed value of all real estate fronting on Notre Dame Street, the said assessed value as set forth and established in and by the Assessment Books for the year one thousand eight hundred and sixty-four, shall be made and levied upon the proprietors of real estate fronting on Notre Dame Street aforesaid, which said Special Assessment shall be due and payable on the *fifteenth day of May instant*, and applied towards the payment of the said sum of *fifty-six thousand three hundred and eighty dollars thirty-four cents*, being one-half of the cost of widening the *third* and portions of the *fourth* Section of Notre Dame Street, as aforesaid.

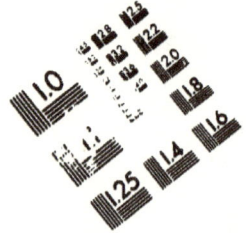

**IMAGE EVALUATION
TEST TARGET (MT-3)**

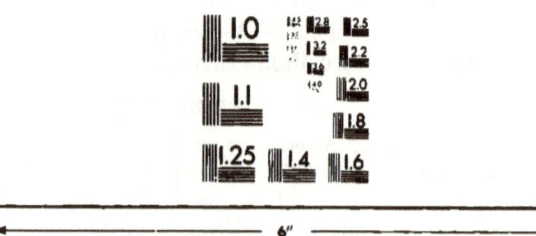

Photographic
Sciences
Corporation

23 WEST MAIN STREET
WEBSTER, N.Y. 14580
(716) 872-4503

No. 11.

By-law concerning the Organization of the Fire Department.

[*Passed* 8*th May* 1867.]

Repealed, see By-law No. 34.

No. 12.

By-law to amend By-law chapter nineteen, concerning Public Markets and the sale of meats, vegetables, &c.

[*Passed* 11*th June* 1867.]

Farmers selling potatoes by the bag to be licensed.

Sec. 1. The fifteenth Section of By-law chapter nineteen, concerning Public Markets and the sale of Meats, Vegetables, &c. passed on the tenth day of May one thousand eight hundred and sixty-five, is hereby amended by striking out the last proviso therein contained, and substituting the following in its stead:—" Provided also that Farmers or Gar-
" deners may sell and deliver to their customers in
" any part of the City, Poultry, Butter, Eggs, Potatoes
" and other Vegetables, and Fruit, upon their obtai-
" ning from the Chief of Police a licence for each
" vehicle used for that purpose, for which they shall
" pay according to the rates specified in the third
" class of licences, as specified in the Tariff of rates
" embodied in the last section of By-law Chapter

" thirty two concerning vehicles; and which said
" licence shall be renewed every year."

Sec. 2. The *twenty-sixth* Section of the said By-law chapter nineteen is hereby repealed.

No. 13.

By-law to impose a special Rate or Assessment on Real Estate in the City of Montreal for School purposes.

[*Passed 20th April* 1868.]

Repealed, see By-law No. 20.

No. 14.

By-law to levy a Special assessment on real estate in Notre Dame Street.

[*Passed 20th April* 1868.]

Preamble:—A Special Assessment at the rate of *one dollar and twenty-five cents and a half* for every *one hundred dollars* of the assessed value of all real estate fronting on Notre Dame Street, the said assessed value as set forth and established in and by the Assessment Books for the year one thousand eight hundred and sixty-four, shall be made and levied upon the proprietors of real estate fronting on Notre Dame Street, aforesaid; which said Special Assessment shall be due and payable on the *fifteenth day of May next*, and applied towards the payment of {.margin Special assessment.}

the said sum of *twenty-eight thousand and five dollars and fifty one cents and a half*, being one-half the cost of widening the Fourth Section of Notre Dame Street, after deducting the sums paid to proprietors who anticipated the improvement, as aforesaid

---

No. 15.

By-Law Concerning Scavengers.

[*Passed 20th May* 1868.]

Repealed,—See By-Law No 46.

No. 16.

By-law concerning Sinks, Privies and Cess-Pools.

[*Passed 9th June* 1868.]

Repealed,—See By-Law No 40.

No. 17.

By-law to change the level of Little St. James Street.

[*Passed 26th August* 1868.]

Preamble.   WHEREAS, it is found advisable to widen Little St. James Street, and it is expedient, in consequence, to change the level of the said street.

It is hereby ordained and enacted by the said Council, and the said Council do hereby ordain and enact :—

That the level of Little St. James Street shall be and the same is hereby altered as follows, except in so far as it relates to the sidewalk on the south-east side of said little St. James street, which, for the present at least, will remain as it is; viz:— Level altered

1. Commencing at a point eighty-six feet to the south of the centre of Little St. James street and Place d'Armes Hill, from thence descending to the centre of Place d'Armes Hill and Little St. James street, where the centre line of the street as widened, will be lowered sixty-nine hundredths of a foot below the present surface of the existing street; thence up an ascending grade of one foot and seventy-six hundredths of a foot per hundred feet, for a distance of three hundred feet, the average depth of cutting between these points being two feet and five-tenths of a foot; thence down a descending grade of a foot per hundred feet, for a distance of two hundred and sixty feet, the average depth of cutting between these points being two feet and seventy-three hundredths of a foot: thence up an ascending grade of seven hundredths of a foot per hundred feet, for a distance of forty-seven feet, the average depth of cutting between these points being two feet and fifty-nine hundredths of a foot; thence up an ascending grade of two feet and thirty-five hundredths of a foot per hundred feet, for a distance of three hundred and thirteen feet, the average depth of cutting between these points being about two feet and one-tenth of a foot. Alteration defined.

2. Commencing at the centre of St. Lambert Hill and Fortification Lane, thence up an ascending grade of eleven feet and forty-three hundredths of a foot

per hundred feet. for a distance of seventy feet, the average depth of filling between these points being about one foot, thence up an ascending grade of five feet and five hundredths of a foot per hundred feet, for a distance of forty-seven feet, the average depth of the filling between these points being one foot, thence up an ascending grade of five feet and five hundredths of a foot per hundred feet for a distance of forty-eight feet, the average depth of cutting between these points being about one foot, thence up an ascending grade of four feet and twenty seven hundredths of a foot per hundred feet for a distance of seventy-five feet, the depth of cutting between these points being about one foot. The whole being in accordance with and as more fully shown on the section of the improvement deposited in the City Surveyor's Office.

The whole of the above dimensions are in English feet and decimals.

No. 18.

By-law to Repeal By-law Number Thirteen, and to impose a special rate or assessment on Real Estate in the said City, for School purposes.

[*Passed* 11*th November*, 1868.]

(Repealed,—see By-Law No 20)

No. 19.

By-law to prohibit the keeping of Pigs within certain sections of the City of Montreal.

[*Passed 15th December* 1868.]

(Repealed— see By-Law No 44.)

No. 20.

By-Law of the Council of the City of Montreal to impose a Special Tax or Assessment on Real Estate, in the said City, for School purposes.

[*Passed 30th April* 1869.]

WHEREAS, it is provided in and by a certain Act passed at the last Session of the Legislature of the " Province of Quebec, intituled "An Act to amend " the law respecting Education in this Province," " that the Corporations of the Cities of Quebec and " Montreal shall pay annually for the support of " the schools in the said Cities a sum equal to three " times the amount of the share of the Government " grant coming to the Schools of the said Cities un- " der the provisions of the said Act"; And Where- " as it is further enacted in and by the said Act, " that "the Corporations of the Cities of Quebec and " Montreal shall levy annually by assessment on " real estate in the said Cities a tax sufficient to

Preamble.

98 BY-LAWS.

" cover the amount payable by them for the sup-
" port of Schools under the provisions of the said
" Act."

It is hereby ordained and enacted by the said Council and the said Council do hereby ordain and enact, as follows:

Special Tax. SEC. 1. An annual tax of eight cents for every one hundred dollars of the assessed value of real estate in the said City of Montreal is hereby imposed on all real estate lying, and being within the said City of Montreal, liable to assessment under the provisions of the said above first-cited Act, over and above all existing rates, taxes or assesments already imposed by the By-Laws of the said Council; and the proceeds of the said special tax shall be applied exclusively to the support of schools in the said city, according to law.

When due. Sec. 2. The said special tax shall become due and payable annually by the owner or owners of real estate in the said City liable to assessment under the provisions of the said above first cited act, from the first day of May, so soon as the return of the Assessment Roll for the several Wards of the said City of Montreal, respectively, shall have been made to the City-Treasurer.

Where payable. Sec. 3. The said special tax or assessment shall be payable at the office of the Treasurer of the said City of Montreal, and, in default of payment of the same shall be recovered in the same manner as the annual assessment in the said City of Montreal for Municipal purposes.

Sec. 4. The By-Law, Number Eighteen passed by the said Council on the eleventh day of November last is hereby repealed. *Repeal.*

No. 21.

By-law to define the duties of the Auditor.

[*Passed 30th April* 1869.]

Sec. 1. The Auditor for the City of Montreal shall be the general accountant for the City, and shall receive and preserve in his office all City account Books, and all Vouchers, documents and papers relating to the accounts and contracts of the City, its revenue, debt and fiscal affairs. *Auditor's title.*

Sec. 2. It shall be his duty to obtain from the City Clerk a certified statement of the annual appropriations, so soon as these pass the Council, in each year, and to open in an Appropriation Ledger, to be by him kept for that purpose, an account for each ; and all warrants, drawn by Committees, shall be charged in deduction of their various appropriations and certified correct before payment. *His duties.*

Sec. 3. He shall not certify for payment any warrant for a purpose unprovided for by appropriation or which may be drawn for an amount exceeding the appropriation. *Payment of warrants regulated.*

Sec. 4. He shall not certify for payment any warrant for a sum or account not previously passed and sanctioned by the Committee, in whose name such warrant is drawn, nor unless such warrant be signed by at least three members of such Committee, *Ibid.*

and countersigned by the Head of the Department therein concerned; with the exception of the regular Pay Lists of the various departments, and petty disbursements therein, which may be certified before being submitted to the respective committees; provided the said pay lists and disbursements are in accordance with appropriations; and all warrants shall have the various accounts they are drawn for attached thereto for the purposes of such certification and fyling on record.

Shall furnish statements to Chairmen.

Sec. 5. It shall be the duty of the Auditor at least once a month, to furnish the Chairmen of Committees and Heads of Departments with the statements of their respective appropriations and expenditure.

Shall inspect books and accounts.

Sec. 6. The Auditor shall, once a month, and oftener if required, make a personal inspection of the books and accounts kept by all officers of the Corporation charged in any manner with the receipt or collection of the City revenues, and shall see that they are well and correctly kept; he shall carefully examine and check all returns made by such officers and certify the same with his initials, if found correct. He shall also require of all such officers in receipt of City moneys, that they shall submit reports thereof with vouchers into the City treasury as often as may be deemed necessary by the Finance Committee; and if any such officer shall refuse or neglect to make an adjustment of his accounts, when so required, as aforesaid, and to pay over such moneys so received, it shall be the duty of the Auditor to communicate the fact to the City Treasurer who shall thereupon issue a notice in writing, directed to such officer, requiring him to immediately make settle-

Defaulters.

ment of his said accounts, and to pay over the balance of moneys in his hands belonging to the City; and in case of the refusal or neglect of such officer to adjust his said accounts, and to pay over said balance, as required, it shall then be the duty of the City Treasurer to make report of the delinquency of such officer to the Mayor who shall at once suspend him from office.

Sec. 7. At the end of each month, and oftener if required, the Auditor shall make out and submit to the Finance Committee, through the City Treasurer a statement showing the amount expended by each Committee and the balance of appropriation remaining at their credit; he shall also report to the Finance Committee, from time to time, through the same channel, any information concerning his department which it may be necessary to bring under their notice. *Statements to be submitted to Finance Com.*

Sec. 8. He shall keep a Registration Ledger of all Stock, Bonds or Debentures which may be issued by the city, separate and distinct from the General Ledger, and also of all transfers or assignments of such Stock, Bonds or Debentures which may from time to time be made; and he shall compare the same with the Books of record kept by the City Clerk and by the City Treasurer respectively. *Registration Ledger to be kept.*

Sec. 9. It shall be his duty, at the end of each month, to compare the cash in Treasury with the balance appearing in the general cash Book, and to enter in a book to be by him kept for that purpose, the component parts of such balance, which shall be, monthly, submitted to the Finance Committee. *Cash in treasury to be compared.*

Chief officers to furnish certain statements.

Sec. 10. It shall be his duty, at the close of each civic year, to furnish the chief officers of the various civic departments with a statement of their expenditure for the past twelve months; and it shall be the duty of the said officers to furnish him with detailed estimates of the requirements of their several departments for the ensuing year, in the following form, to wit:—

1. For general and ordinary expenditure:
2. For any proposed additions to the same:
3. For contemplated improvements and new work:

with the view of submitting the same to the Finance Committee before the close of the month of February.

Auditor to furnish abstracts, &c.

Sec. 11. The Auditor, whenever required, shall furnish the Mayor or any Committee of the Council, or the City Treasurer, with abstracts of any books, accounts, records, vouchers, or documents in his office, or any information in relation to any thing pertaining to his office or to the revenue of the city; and he shall at all times permit the Mayor, any Member of the Council, the City Clerk, the City Treasurer, or any other officer interested, to examine any books, papers or documents in his office.

Shall render any other services.

Sec. 12. The Auditor shall render any other services or perform any other duties, as the City Council or the Finance Committee may, from time to time, direct.

Repeal.

Sec. 13. The By-Law, number nine, passed by the Council of the said City of Montreal, on the

Fourth day of February, One Thousand Eight Hundred and Sixty-seven, is hereby repealed.

No. 22.
By-law concerning Dogs.
(Passed 7 June 1869.)

(Repealed, see By-law No. 33.)

No. 23.
By-law concerning the Sale of Milk.
(Passed 7th June 1869.)

(Repealed. See By-Law No. 38.)

No. 24.
By-law to repeal Section Second of By-law Chapter Twenty Nine, concerning streets.
(Passed 14th June 1869.)

(Repealed. See By-Law No. 48.)

No. 25.
By-law to amend By-law Number seventeen, to change the Level of Little St. James Street.
(Passed 14th June 1869.)

WHEREAS, it was found advisable in and by the Preamble. By-Law Number Seventeen, passed by the Council of the City of Montreal on the Twenty-Sixth day of August last past, to change the level of Little St. James Street, except in so far as it relates to the sidewalk on the south-east side of said Little St. James Street; and, whereas, Joseph A. Labadie, Esq., one of the proprietors on the said south-east side of Little St. James Street is about to build, and has expressed his desire to conform with the new level of the said street, as established by the said By-Law number Seventeen.

It is hereby ordained and enacted by the said Council, and the said Council do hereby ordain and enact as follows :—

<small>Provices level altered in a certain case.</small> The level of said Little St. James Street established by the said By-Law Number Seventeen, shall apply to and extend as far as the line of the property of the said Joseph A. Labadie, on the south-east side of the said street, as shown and specified in the plan or section hereunto annexed.

No. 26.

By-law to regulate the planting of Trees in certain streets of the City.

(Passed 14th March 1869.)

<small>Preamble.</small> WHEREAS, in and by the twenty-sixth Section of the Act of the Province of Quebec, passed in the thirty-second year of Her Majesty's Reign, Chapter 70, power is conferred upon the Corporation of this City to pass a By-law concerning the plantation of trees within the limits of the City.

BY-LAWS.

It is hereby ordained and enacted by the said Council, and the said Council do hereby ordain and enact, as follows:—

Sec. 1. Every owner of real estate, situated on the Streets mentioned in the Schedule hereunto annexed, shall henceforth be held and obliged to plant on and along his property, trees, at a distance of not more than thirty nor less than fifteen feet from one another, of the quality and in the manner to be prescribed by the City Surveyor, under the direction of the Road Committee. *Proprietors held to plant trees.*

Sec. 2. In case such owner, after having been notified by the said City Surveyor to plant trees, as prescribed in the preceding section, shall neglect to comply with such notice within eight days from the service of the same, or shall refuse to follow the said City Surveyor's instructions, the latter shall cause such plantation to be made, and shall exact and recover the cost thereof from the said owner. *What? in case of refusal.*

Sec. 3. The City Surveyor may order the pruning or trimming of any trees in the public streets or squares, when required. *Pruning of trees.*

Schedule of Streets wherein Trees are to be planted, referred to in the foregoing By-Law.

EAST WARD.—Jacques Cartier Square, Dalhousie Square. *Streets in which trees are to be planted.*

ST. ANN'S WARD.—William, Wellington, (beyond the Bridge), St. Patrick, McCord, Guy, Richmond, St. Martin.

ST. ANTOINE WARD.—St. Radegonde, Aylmer, City Councillors, Union Avenue, Brunswick, Hanover, University, Albert (S. E. side), Latour (West), Upper Stanley, Victoria, McGill College Avenue, Mansfield, Metcalfe, Peel, Stanley, Drummond, Mountain, Crescent, Guy, St. François de Salles, Sherbrooke, Dorchester, McTavish, Redpath, St. Janvier, Simpson, Berthelet, Cathcart, Lagauchetière, St. Antoine, Inspector (from St. Bonaventure to St. Antoine), Beaver Hall place, Burnside Place, Victoria Square, Phillip's Square.

St. Lawrence Ward.—Upper Bleury, Durocher, Sherbrooke, Hotel Dieu, Ontario, St. Catherine, Craig.

St. Louis Ward.—Sherbrooke, Ontario, St. Catherine, Dorchester, Craig, St. Elizabeth (above Sherbrooke), Cadieux, Courville, Upper St. Urbain, Ste. Famille, Manse.

St. James Ward.—Amherst, St. Hubert, St. Denis, Berri, Sherbrooke, Ontario, Ste. Catherine, Mignonne, Lagauchetière.

St. Mary's Ward.—Fullum, Seaton, Sydenham, Durham, Ste. Catherine, Ontario, Dorchester, Craig.

No. 27

By-law to Amend By-law Chapter Six in relation to Assessments and Taxes.

[*Passed 15th December* 1869.]

Sec. 1. The *Sixteenth* Section of the said By-law Chapter Six, is hereby repealed, and the following substituted therefor.

Every person or firm of persons carrying on the business or occupation of livery stable keeper, for the purpose of letting out horses or vehicles of travel for hire or reward in the said city shall pay the duty imposed in and by the *Seventh* Section of the said By-law, Chapter Six, and a further annual duty at the rate of Three Dollars for every two-wheeled vehicle or carriage and at the rate of four dollars for every four-weeled vehicle or carriage kept for the purposes aforesaid; which said duties shall, for the current year, be due and payable on the twentieth day of December instant, and thereafter on the first day of May in each and every year. Tax on livery stable keepers amended

Sec. 2. The *thirty-second* and *thirty-third* sections of the said By-law, Chapter Six, are hereby repealed, and the following substituted therefor: Repeal.

An annual duty of eighty Dollars is hereby imposed upon all brokers, money lenders or changers, commission merchants, and the agents of all such in this city; and the said duty shall, for the current year, be due and payable on the twentieth day of December instant, and thereafter on the first day of May in each and every year. Tax on Brokers.

No. 28.

By-law to fix and regulate the hours for the opening and closing of Taverns, Dram-Shops, Saloons, and other houses or places of Public entertainment in this City. *

(Passed 9th, February 1870.)

Hours fixed for closing taverns, &c.
Sec. 1. No person keeping any Inn, Tavern, Public Billiard Room, Saloon, Dram-shop, Hotel, or other house or place of public entertainment in the City of Montreal, shall keep open such Inn, Tavern, Public Billiard Room, Saloon, Dram-shop, Hotel or other house or place of public entertainment, nor permit tippling or drinking of spirituous or fermented liquors therein, after the hour of eleven o'clock at night and before six o'clock in the morning, from the first day of October to the thirty-first day of March in each year; and after the hour of twelve o'clock at night and before five o'clock in the morning, between the first day of April and the thirtieth day of September, in each year.

Tippling prohibited &c
Sec. 2. It shall not be lawful for any person to tipple or drink spirituous or fermented liquors in any Inn, Tavern, Public Billiard Room, Saloon, Dram-Shop, Hotel or other house or place of public entertainment, during the hours prohibited in and by the foregoing Section.

---

* Sanctioned by the Lieutenant Governor on the 25th February 1870.

Sec. 3. All persons offending against any of the provisions of this By-Law shall be liable to a penalty of not less than ten dollars, nor more than twenty dollars, and the costs of the prosecution ; and, in default of immediate payment of the said fine and costs, to an imprisonment of not less than one nor more than two months, unless the said fine and costs shall be sooner paid. *Penalty.*

No. 29.

By-law to impose a Duty on Billiard Tables.

[Passed 15th March, 1870.]

Sec. 1. The thirty-ninth section of the By-law chapter six of this Council is hereby repealed, and the following section substituted in its stead :— *39 sec. of By-Law c. 6 repealed.*

Sec. 2. An Annual duty of one hundred dollars shall be paid by the occupant or occupants, proprietor or proprietors of each and every House of Public Entertainment, Hotel, Inn, Licensed Tavern, Public Boarding House, or any other place of public resort, entertainment or amusement whatever in the said City, for one Billiard Table; of fifty dollars for the second Billiard Table, and of twenty for each and every additional Billiard Table, and of one hundred dollars for each and every Mississippi, Bagatelle or any other gambling Board with Balls, which now is or may hereafter be erected or kept in any such House of Public Entertainment, Hotel, Inn, or Licensed Tavern, Public Boarding House, or other place of public resort, entertainment or *Duty on Billiard Tables.*

amusement; and a duty of one hundred dollars shall be paid by the occupant or proprietor of any house, apartment, or other place, in the said City, for one Billiard Table, of fifty dollars for the second Billiard Table, and of twenty dollars for each and every additional Billiard Table, and of one hundred dollars for each and every Missisippi, Bagatelle, or other gambling board with balls, which now is or may hereafter be established or kept for the use of any association, or number of subscribers, or for any person whomsoever, other than the said occupant of the said House, apartment or other place; and a duty of twenty dollars shall be paid by all legally established and incorporated Clubs, for each and every Billiard Table which they may own or have the exclusive use of; and any person, occupant, proprietor, as the case may be who shall set up, erect or keep a Billiard table, Missisippi, Bagatelle, or any other gambling board with balls, without having previously paid the said annual duty, according to the respective rates herein before specified, shall be liable to a fine not exceeding twenty dollars and costs of prosecution, and in default of immediate payment of the said fine and costs, the defendant may be imprisoned in the common goal for a period not exceeding two months, the said imprisonment to cease upon payment of the said fine and costs.

Billiards used by Clubs.

No. 30.

By-law in relation to the Manufacture and Sale of Bread.

[Passed 15th March 1870.]

Sec. 1. All Bread manufactured by the Bakers of this City for sale, shall be made of the weight and quality hereinafter described, that is to say : the brown loaf shall be made of good wholesome wheaten flour, and be baked in loaves of six pounds avoirdupois weight each, or of half-loaves of three pounds avoirdupois weight each ; the white loaf shall be made of good sound fine wheaten flour, and shall be baked in loaves of four pounds avoirdupois weight each ; or of half-loaves of two pounds avoirdupois weight each ; and every loaf of such Bread shall be marked with the numbers indicating the weight of such loaf, and also with the initial letters of the name of the Baker or Bakers thereof. And if any Baker or other person, or company of persons, shall bake, expose, or offer for sale, in the said City, any wheaten loaves of less weight than such as hereinbefore described, or than what the said loaf or loaves purport to be, or that shall be made of unwholesome materials, calculated to defraud the public, or any loaf or loaves not marked as aforesaid, every such Baker or other person or Company so offending, shall be liable to a fine not exceeding twenty dollars and costs of prosecution and to an imprisonment not exceeding two months, for each offence, and shall moreover suffer the forfeiture and confiscation of all such

_{Weight and quality of bread.}

_{Mark indicative of weight and initial letters of baker's name.}

_{Penalty.}

_{Confiscation.}

Proviso.

Bread as shall be found of light weight, or of an inferior quality, or not marked as aforesaid : Provided always that such deficiency in the weight of such Bread shall be ascertained by the Inspector or Inspectors of Bread, to be appointed by the said Council, by weighing or causing the same to be weighed in his or their presence, within eight hours after the same shall have been baked, sold, or exposed for sale : And provided further, that whenever any allowance in the weight shall be claimed on account of any bread having been baked, sold, or exposed for sale since more than eight hours as aforesaid, the burden of proof in respect to the time when the same shall have been baked, sold, or exposed for sale, shall devolve upon the Defendant or Baker of such Bread.

Proviso.

Council to appoint Inspectors of Bread.

Their duties.

Sec. 2. It shall be lawful for the Council of the said City from time to time, as occasion may require, to appoint one or more fit person or persons to be Inspector or Inspectors of Bread ; and it shall be the duty of the said Inspector or Inspectors, and they are hereby authorized and required from time to time, not less than once in each month and whenever ordered so to do by the Mayor of the said City, at all seasonable hours, to enter into, and inspect and examine every Baker's shop, store, house, or other building where any Bread is or shall be baked, stored, or deposited, or offered for sale, and in the presence of at least one witness, to inspect, weigh, and examine all Bread found therein ; and also to stop, detain, and examine in any part of the said City, any person or persons, or any waggons or other vehicles carrying any loaf or loaves for sale, and in the presence, as aforesaid, of at least one witness, to weigh the same, and determine whether the same are in violation of the true intent and meaning of the present By-law ; and if the said Inspector or any one or more of the said Inspectors shall find any loaf or loaves of Bread deficient in weight or not conformable to the directions herein contained or any part of them, he or they shall immediately seize and confiscate the same for distribution to the poor.

Sec. 3. If any Baker or other person shall hinder, obstruct, or prevent any Inspector or Inspectors of Bread, from making any examination authorized or required of him or them by this By-law ; or shall hinder, obstruct or prevent any Inspector or Inspectors aforesaid, or any person aiding or assisting him or them, from stopping any waggon or other vehicle for carrying Bread ; or from seizing, taking and carrying away, and disposing of, according to law, any Bread found in the said City, not conformable to this Bylaw ; every person so offending shall be liable to a fine not exceeding twenty dollars and costs of prosecution and to an imprisonment not exceeding two months, for each offence. *Penalty for obstructing Inspectors of Bread in the execution of their duty.*

No. 31

By-law concerning the erection of Buildings.

[Passed 15th March 1870.]

Sec. 1. The Inspector of Buildings appointed to enforce the laws relating to the construction of Buildings in this City, and for the prevention of *Title of Inspector.*

accidents by fire, shall be termed *Inspector of Buildings*, and shall be under the direction of the Fire Committee.

Wooden buildings and shingled roofs prohibited.

Sec. 2. No person shall hereafter construct any Wooden Building, of any kind or description whatever, within the limits of the said City ; or cover wholly or in part any Building of any kind whatsoever, within the City limits, except as hereinafter provided, with shingles or wooden material of any kind whatsoever ; neither shall any person erect or construct, or attach to any building, within the limits aforesaid, any gutter, conductor, or spout that is not effectually secured against fire. It may however be lawful to erect Buildings encased with brick work. Provided, however, that nothing in this law contained shall be construed in any manner to prevent the Council of this said City, in special cases, and for special causes, to give permission to erect buildings different from those specified in the next preceding section.

Proviso.

Buildings now supported.

Sec. 3. No front, rear, or other wall of any such dwelling house, Store, Storehouse or other Building now erected, or hereafter to be erected, in the said City, shall be cut off or altered below, to be supported in any manner in whole or in part by wood, but shall be wholly supported by stone, brick, or iron, and no wood, shall be used between such wall and such supporters.

Wooden buildings a nuisance.

Sec. 4. Every building hereafter erected or constructed contrary to the provisions of the foregoing sections, shall be, and the same is hereby declared to be a public and common nuisance.

Sec. 5. No person shall repair, or cause to be repaired, any wooden or other roof of any brick or stone house or building, or any spout, belonging or attached to any house or building within this City with any shingles, boards, planks, or other wooden materials whatsoever ; or with any other than metal or incombustible materials. *Wooden roofs or spouts not to be repaired with shingles or boards.*

Sec. 6. But whereas it has been shown to the satisfaction of the City Council, that the compositions for covering the roofs of buildings, known and patented as "Warren's Prepared Fire and Waterproof Composition Roofing," and " Racicot and Laurent's prepared Fire and Water-proof Composition Roofing," are really and truly fire-proof, it may be lawful to construct board and plank roofs to buildings within the limits of this City, and to cover the same with either of the said compositions : Provided, however, that the Inspector of buildings shall be empowered to order the same to be removed and to be replaced with metal in case of roofs so covered which he shall decide to be defective and liable to damage by fire. *Certain compositions for roofing permitted. Proviso.*

Sec. 7. If any wooden building shall require new roofing, it shall and may be lawful for the proprietor or proprietors thereof to raise the same for the purpose of making a flat roof, provided that such new roof shall be covered with metal or any of the articles sanctioned to be used in the next preceding section of this by-law, and provided such building when so raised shall not exceed thirty-five feet in height to the highest part thereof from the curb level. *Wooden buildings may receive a new roof, &c.*

Sec. 8. No Wooden building now erected shall be enlarged or built upon, unless such extension or addition be of fireproof materials, nor shall any Wooden Building be removed from one lot to another.

May be enlarged.

Sec. 9. No Wooden Shed shall be erected or permitted unless one whole side of the same shall be left entirely and constantly open, and provided also the same does not exceed twelve feet in height to the peak or highest part thereof from the level upon which it is placed. Nothing in this section or in this By-law shall be held or construed to prohibit the erection of any Piazza, Platform or Balcony, not to exceed ten feet in width on the level of the first story of any Building to which the same may be attached: provided that such Piazza, Platform or Balcony shall not extend more than three feet above the second floor of any such Building as aforesaid.

Wooden sheds.

Piazza, balconies, &c.

Sec. 10. All Privies not exceeding ten feet square and ten feet high shall, and all Ferry-houses may, be built and covered with wood, provided such Privies and Ferry-houses shall not be used for any other purpose than a Privy or Ferry-house.

Privies, &c.

Sec. 11. Every Wooden Building, which may hereafter be damaged by fire to an amount less than one half of its value, may be repaired or rebuilt; but if such damage be greater than one-half such value thereof, then such Building shall not be repaired or rebuilt, but shall be taken down.

Repairs to wooden buildings.

Sec. 12. The amount and extent of such damage by fire or otherwise, mentioned in the last preceding section, shall be determined by the Inspector

Damage, by whom ascertained.

of Buildings, one Surveyor appointed by the Fire Insurance Company or Companies, if such Building be insured, and one by the owner, or owners of the property. But if such Building or Buildings be not insured, then the damage shall be determined by the said Inspector, one person appointed by the owner or owners, and another expert chosen by the two former. In case the owner or owners, shall refuse or neglect to appoint an expert for the purpose of estimating such damage, then it shall be lawful for the Recorder to appoint such expert.

Sec. 13. No person or persons shall hereafter construct in any House or Building covered with shingles, or wood, within the said City, any Chimney or Chimneys which shall be elevated less than three feet six inches above the ridge-pole thereof, or shall construct in any house covered with metal, slate, or tile, any Chimney or Chimneys which shall be so elevated less than two feet, or shall construct such Chimney or Chimneys so obliquely as to prevent it or them being easily swept, or shall construct any vent or vents or sweep opening in such Chimney or Chimneys of less area than one hundred and forty-four inches each, or shall fail to have the joints of the bricks, when such material is employed, smoothly pointed or drawn, the bricks also to be well laid in mortar, and grouted with liquid mortar. *Construction of chimneys.*

Sec. 14. No person shall hereafter construct, or permit to be constructed, in his, or her house, in the said City, any Chimney of brick, the sides of which shall be of less thickness than eight inches, within such Building, and the area of the flue *Brick chimneys, &c.*

thereof less than one hundred and forty-four inches, or without having a good and proper stone foundation; neither shall any person pass a stove-pipe through the top or sides of any Wooden-house, Out-house, Fence, or any Building whatsoever, owned or occupied by such person in the said City.

Stove-pipe through roof.

Sec. 15. Any proprietor or proprietors of any House or Building within the said City, who shall neglect or refuse to maintain the Chimney or Chimneys of such House or Building in good condition, or to repair the same, when required by the Inspector aforesaid, or fail to cause the removal of any obstruction or obstructions in the said Chimney or Chimneys, preventing the same from being well and easily swept, or who shall permit more than two pipes to terminate in the same Chimney in each story of such House or Building, or who shall allow a stove-pipe to terminate in any other place than in a Chimney, shall incur and pay the penalty hereinafter provided.

Chimneys to be kept in order, &c.

Sec. 16. The proprietor or proprietors of any House or Building within the said City, having any Chimney or Chimneys with no fire-place or fire-places thereto, shall cause to be made into such Chimney or Chimneys such opening or openings, securely guarded by iron doors and frames, as shall admit the said Chimney or Chimneys to be easily swept: said iron doors to be at least twelve inches square.

Chimneys without fire-places.

Sec. 17. All Ladders to Chimneys in the said City shall hereafter be well secured and fastened to the same by iron hooks, and shall not extend higher than within six inches from the tops of such Chim-

Ladders to chimneys.

neys; and the tops of Chimneys, if composed of brick, or more than one stone, shall be hooped with iron.

Sec. 18. It shall be the duty of the proprietor, or in case the proprietor is absent, of the occupant or any person having the care of any House or Building in the said city to have and maintain on such House or Building, a sufficient number of ladders and to have the same repaired or renewed when required by the said Inspector. *Ladders on buildings.*

Sec. 19. The gable ends of all houses to be hereafter built in the said City, shall be elevated at least two feet above the roof thereof, and the coping or covering of such gables shall be made of stone or covered with metal. *Gable ends of houses.*

Sec. 20. No person shall hereafter lay, or permit to be laid or placed in any wooden floor, any hearth, brick or stone, which shall not rest upon brick or stone underneath to its whole extent, not less than three inches in thickness, and which shall not be well bedded in mortar, and grouted so as to fill all the spaces, said brick or stone hearth to be eight inches longer at each end than the fire-place, and sixteen inches in width from the face of the Chimney. *Placing of hearth-stones.*

Sec. 21. All proprietors of Houses or Buildings adjoining any public square, street, lane, or highway within the said city, shall have and maintain to such Houses or Buildings, tight covered spouts, by which the water from the roofs of such Houses or Buildings may be conveyed to within a distance of not greater than twelve inches from the footpath or sidewalk: Provided always, that in case of the *Buildings adjoining streets to have spouts.* *Proviso.*

absence of such proprietors, the occupants shall be held responsible in the premises, for each offence against the provisions of this section.

Wooden beams or supporters.

Sec. 22. No person shall hereafter use or employ any wooden beam or post of any kind or description whatever, or cause the same to be used or employed to permanently sustain, uphold or support any brick or stone wall of any house within the said City, unless said beam or post shall be made of ash, oak, or elm, and be at least twelve inches square.

Beams in walls.

Sec. 23. No person shall hereafter build or enter, or permit to be built or entered, any beam or joist into any wall in his House or Building, in the said City, nearer than eight inches to any flue or fire-place in such wall, and all such beams or joists shall be entered into trimmers, framed so as to be at least one inch clear of all Chimneys and flues. All beams and other timbers in the party wall or every such Dwelling-house, Store, Store-house or other building, hereafter to be erected or built as aforesaid, shall be separated from the beam or timber entering in the opposite side of the wall by at least four inches of solid mason work. No person shall place any stove for burning wood into any partition in the said house, without leaving nine inches clear from any wood work immediately above such stove, and seven inches clear from any wood work opposite the sides of the same; and all stoves whether to burn wood or coal, shall be placed upon metal plates, or pans projecting at least eighteen inches beyond the door of said stove.

Stoves.

Coal stoves.

Sec. 24. No person shall place any stove for burning coal in any partition in the said house without leaving eighteen inches of clear space on all sides, unless said partition shall be protected by tin plate, nor shall any coal stove be placed nearer to any wooden partition or wood work of any kind than two feet, unless said wood work shall be protected by a screen of tin plate.

Sec. 25. Any proprietor of any House, Store, or other Building within the said City, more than one story high, who shall neglect to have and maintain an aperture, scuttle, or dormer window of not less dimensions than four hundred and thirty-two inches in area, on the roof thereof, with a ladder or steps thereto, or shall refuse to construct such scuttle or stairs within two weeks after being notified so to do by the said Inspector, shall incur and pay the penalty hereinafter provided. *Scuttles on roofs.*

Sec. 26. Every building, except a private dwelling, over thirty and under fifty feet in width, shall have at least one brick or stone wall running from front to rear ; or if over fifty feet and under seventy-five feet width, shall have two partition walls as above ; or if over seventy feet and under one hundred feet, shall have three partition walls as above. *Partition walls.*

Sec. 27. In all other cases not hereinbefore specified, wherever the said Inspector shall detect any imperfection, improper construction, or defect in any house or building within the said City, from which imperfection, improper construction, or defect there may apparently be danger from fire, the proprietor of such house or building shall repair or remedy the same, within a reasonable time after being notified so to do by the said Inspector. Pro- *Imperfections in the construction of houses.*

vided always, that in case of the absence of such proprietor, the occupant, or any person having the care of such house or building, shall be held responsible for each offence against the provisions of this section.

Prohibition extended to repairs.

Sec. 28. The same prohibitions and conditions which are hereby enacted as applicable to new Buildings, shall be held to apply also to the repairs of Buildings already erected.

Inspector may enter buildings, &.

Sec. 29. The Inspector of Buildings shall have the right to enter all Buildings and premises on all lawful days, and during seasonable hours, for the purpose of performing the duties appertaining to his office.

Scaffolds how to be constructed.

Sec. 30. All Scaffolds erected in this City for use in the erection or repair of stone, brick, or other Buildings, shall be well and safely supported, and of sufficient width, and properly secured, so as to insure the safety of persons working thereon, or passing under or by the same, against the falling thereof, or of such materials as may be used, placed, or deposited thereon; and any person who shall erect, or use, or cause to be erected or used any Scaffold contrary to the provisions hereof, shall be subject to the penalty hereinafter provided.

Dilapidated walls, &c., to be pulled down.

Sec. 31. It shall be the duty of the Inspector of Buildings to require, by a written or printed notice, that all dilapidated or ruinous Walls, Chimneys, or Buildings, that may endanger the public safety, be pulled down, demolished, and removed by the owner or party in possession, or having charge thereof, within a reasonable delay, varying according to the circumstances of each case, and to be specified in the said notice; and every person on whom such notice shall be served, shall forthwith obey and comply with the requirements thereof.

Sec. 32. When the person on whom notice shall have been served as aforesaid, shall refuse, or neglect to obey, or comply with the requirements thereof, it shall be lawful for the said Inspector, at the expense of the party notified, to pull down, demolish and remove, or to cause to be pulled down, demolished and removed, all such dilapidated or ruinous walls, chimneys, or buildings as may be specified or referred to in the said notice, and that may endanger the public safety; provided, however, that such pulling down, demolition, and removal of the said walls, chimneys, or buildings by the said Inspector, shall not exempt the party on whom notice shall have been served as aforesaid, from the hereinafter imposed penalty. *At whose expense.*

Sec. 33. The expense of pulling down, demolishing, and removing any such dilapidated or ruinous Walls, Chimneys, and Buildings, whensoever incurred by the said Inspector, may be recovered with costs in the Recorder's Court, from the owner, or the person in possession or having charge of the said dilapidated or ruinous Walls, Chimneys, or Buildings, refusing or neglecting to pull down or demolish the same as aforesaid. *Ibid.*

Sec. 34. Whereas serious accidents have occurred, and much danger may be apprehended from the want of proper precautions being taken to prevent the loss of life by fire in Public Halls, Churches, or other Buildings wherein large assemblies usually gather: Be it therefore enacted, that no Lecture *Public buildings to be provided with means for the safe egress of assemblies in case of accident.*

Hall, Theatre, Concert or Ball Room, Church, or other like Building in the said City, shall be used for the convening of assemblies of more than one hundred persons, unless the same be so constructed as to offer adequate means for the safe egress of such assemblies, in case of any accident by fire, and unless the proprietor or party in charge of the above mentioned Buildings shall have obtained a certificate to that effect from the Inspector of Buildings:

Proviso. Provided that in all cases the entrance doors to such Lecture Halls, Theatres, Concert or Ball Rooms, Churches, or other Buildings shall be of adequate dimensions, and so made and affixed as to open exteriorly.

Duty of Inspector of Buildings. Sec. 35. It shall be the duty of the Inspector of buildings to examine each and every Lecture Hall, Theatre, Concert or Ball Room. Church, or other building as aforesaid, and to notify the owner or person in charge of the same, by a written or printed notice, to comply with the provisions of the next preceding section of this by-law, within a reasonable delay, not to exceed however thirty days ; and any such owner or person in charge of the said buildings who shall refuse or neglect to comply with such provisions, within the delay aforesaid, shall be liable to the following penalty.

Penalty. Sec. 36. Any owner, builder, or other person who shall own, build, or aid in the erection of any building or part of building within this City, contrary to, or in any other manner than authorized by the provisions of this By-law shall be liable to a fine not exceeding twenty dollars and costs of prosecution and to an imprisonment not exceeding two months for each offence. If any person shall violate any other provision of this by-law, he shall be subject to the same penalty.

No. 32.

By-law to regulate the sale and measurement of Coal.

(Passed 15th March 1870.)

Sec. 1. All Anthracite Coal which shall hereafter be sold in this City, shall be sold by weight; and the ton of two thousand pounds avoirdupoids weight with its parts and proportions, shall be held as the weight by which the same shall in all cases (except by cargo) be sold. Anthracite coal to be sold by weight.

Sec. 2. On or before the delivery of such Coal, so sold, it shall be the duty of the seller thereof, unless otherwise mutually agreed upon, to cause the same to be weighed by one of the public weighers hereinafter designated, and a certificate of the weight thereof, signed by the weigher, shall be delivered to the buyer, or his agent, at the time of the delivery of such coal; a duplicate of which certificate shall also be delivered to the seller, or his agent, if required. Ibid. Certificate of weight.

Sec. 3. No person engaged in the business of selling Coal shall act as a weigher under the preceding section. Sellers of coal not to act as weighers.

Sec. 4. Any person who shall offend against the provisions of either of the foregoing sections of this By-law, shall for each and every offence, be liable Penalty.

to a fine not exceeding twenty dollars and costs of prosecution and to an imprisonment not exceeding two months, for each offence.

Who shall act as weighers. Sec. 5. The Clerks of the several Public Markets in this City, with the exception of the Bonsecours and St. Lawrence Markets, shall be, and they are hereby authorised to act as weighers of such Coal, and to receive, on behalf of the said Council, the fees hereinafter mentioned.

Fees for weighing coal. SEC. 6. The following shall be the fees which the said weighers shall be entitled to receive for the weighing of Coal as aforesaid, viz :

For every load of Coal, not exceeding fifteen hundred pounds in weight,—Five cents.

For every load of Coal, exceeding fifteen hundred pounds in weight,—Ten cents; which said fees shall include the certificate (in duplicate) of the weight of such Coal, and shall be paid by the seller thereof; and the said certificate shall contain the gross weight, the tare and the number of the vehicle in which the same was weighed.

Weighers shall submit reports, etc. Sec. 7. The said weighers shall submit to the City Clerk quarterly reports of their doings, in which shall be stated the number of tons and fractions of tons of coal weighed by them respectively, together with the amount of fees received, of which fees they shall make weekly returns to the City Treasurer.

No. 33.

By-law concerning Dogs.

(Passed 15th March 1870.)

SEC. 1. Every owner or keeper of a dog in the City of Montreal shall annually, on or before the thirtieth day of May, cause it to be registered, numbered, described and licensed for one year from the first day of the month of June, in the Office of the Chief of Police of the said City: and shall cause it to wear around its neck a collar, to which shall be attached, by a metallic fastening, a circular metallic plate, having raised or cast thereon the letters C. T. P., and the figures indicating the year for which the tax has been paid, and number corresponding with the number of the Registry on the book in the Office of the Chief of Police; and the said owner or keeper shall pay for such, license Two Dollars for a male dog and Three Dollars for a female dog. Dogs to be licensed, &c. Fee.

SEC. 2. The Chief of Police shall issue the said license, and receive and pay the money therefor in the City Treasury. Chief of Police to issue license.

SEC. 3. Any person becoming the owner or keeper of a dog, not duly licensed, after the thirtieth day of June, shall cause said dog to be registered, numbered, described and licensed until the first day of the month of June, after the ensuing year, in the manner and subject to the terms prescribed in the first section. Persons becoming owners of unlicensed dogs.

SEC. 4. The Chief of Police shall, from and after the first day of July, cause to be killed or destroyed all dogs found going at large in the said City not Unlicensed dogs to be killed.

licensed and collared according to the foregoing provisions.

Valuable dogs may be impounded if unlicensed.

SEC. 5. The Chief of Police may, in his discretion cause any valuable dog remaining at large in any street uncollared and unlicensed, to be impounded in any of the public pounds for forty eight hours, during which the owner of said dog may recover the same on payment of fifty cents, besides the cost of the license; if not reclaimed within that time such dog may be destroyed or sold, and the proceeds of such sale paid over to the City Treasurer.

Licensed dogs to be accompanied by their owners.

SEC. 6. Any licensed dog found running at large in any street, unaccompanied by its owner, may be taken up by the Police and impounded, of which notice shall be given to the owner of such dog, who may recover the same on payment of a fine of fifty cents.

Persons whose dogs are complained of, to be proceeded against.

SEC. 7. On complaint being made to the Chief of Police of this said city, of any dog, licensed or unlicensed, within this said city, which shall, by barking, biting, howling or in any other way or manner disturb the quiet of any person or persons whomsoever, the Chief of Police, on such complaint, shall issue, or cause to be issued, notice thereof to the person keeping or permitting such dog to be kept, or the owner thereof; and in case such person or owner shall, for the space of three days after such notice, neglect to cause such dog to be removed and kept beyond the limits of the city, or to be destroyed, he shall be liable to a fine not exceeding twenty dollars and costs of prosecution, and in default of immediate payment of the said fine and costs, the defendant may be imprisoned in the common gaol for a period not exceeding two months, the said imprisonment to cease upon payment of the said fine and costs; provided, however, that the Recorder's Court, before which such complaint shall be heard and tried, shall be satisfied that such dog had, in manner aforesaid, disturbed the quiet of any person or persons in the said city.

SEC. 8. If any person after being convicted under the provisions of the next preceding section of this By-Law, shall still neglect or refuse to destroy his dog, on being ordered so to do, it shall be the duty of the Chief of Police to cause such dog to be destroyed. Dogs to be destroyed in certain cases.

SEC. 9. Whenever information may be given to the Mayor of the city that a mad dog has been seen running at large in any part of the said city, or in any part of the parish of Montreal, or whenever it shall appear to the said Mayor that there is reason to apprehend danger to the safety of citizens, from mad dogs, it shall be lawful for the said Mayor, and he is hereby authorized to give public notice, enjoining all persons in the said City of Montreal to confine their dogs, or muzzle them in such a manner, as that they shall be totally unable to bite; and that, during a space of time, which shall not exceed two calendar months, to be computed from the date of the publication of the said notice; and the said notice shall mention the time at which the confinement or muzzling of the said dogs shall cease. Mads dogs.

Notice by the Mayor.

SEC. 20. It shall be the duty of the Chief of Police to cause to be destroyed all dogs that may be found Dogs found unmuzzled to be killed.

running at large, or wandering in any part of the said city, not muzzled, in the manner required by the preceding section of this By-Law, after the publication of the said notice, and while the said notice shall continue in force ; and each and every owner, master or person in charge of, or that usually harbours any dog which shall be found running at large, or wandering in any part of the said city, without being muzzled in the manner aforesaid, after such notice shall be published, and while such notice shall continue in force, shall be liable to a fine not exceeding twenty dollars and costs of prosecution and to an imprisonment not exceeding two months, for each offence.

Penalty. SEC. 11. All persons who shall violate, or fail to comply with any of the provisions of this By-Law, to which no penalty is attached in any preceding section of this By-Law, shall be liable to a fine not exceeding Twenty Dollars and costs of prosecution, and in default of immediate payment of the said fine and costs, the defendant may be imprisoned in the common gaol for a period not exceeding two months, the said imprisonment to cease upon payment of the said fine and costs·

Interpretation. SEC. 12. The word "Dog" wherever used in this By-Law, shall be construed and taken in its general sense, and embracing any number of dogs owned or kept by each individual.

Repeal of former provisions. SEC. 13. The By-Law chapter thirteen of the Consolidated By-Laws of the Council of the City of Montreal, and section twenty-four of By-Law chapter six of the said Consolidated By-Laws are repealed.

No. 34.

By-law concerning the organization of the Fire Department.

[*Passed* 15*th March* 1870.]

Sec. 1. The Fire Department of this City shall be under the direction of the Fire Committee of the Council. <small>Fire Dept. under whose direction.</small>

Sec. 2. The Fire Department of this City shall be composed of the undermentioned officers and men, who shall be known and designated as follows:— <small>How constituted.</small>

>One Chief Engineer,
>One Assistant Engineer,
>One Hosemaker and Cleaner,
>Nine Guardians,
>Twenty one Assistant Guardians,

who shall be called the "City Fire Police," and as Firemen shall be entitled to all the privileges, immunities, and exemptions as by law established.

Sec. 3. There shall be a permanent establishment of nine Stations, to be numbered from one to nine, in each of which there shall be placed such a portion of the Fire Department as the Fire Committee may, from time to time, determine, who shall perform all the duties required of them, and especially the protection of property from fire, and the watering of the streets. Each Station shall be supplied with the necessary apparatus and equipment of horses, hose reels, carriages, ladders, axes, torches, etc., etc. <small>Permanent establishment of stations.</small>

Sec 4. It shall be lawful for the said Fire Committee, having first obtained the consent of the <small>Number of stations may be increased.</small>

Council therefor, to add to the present establishment by increasing the number of Stations with men and equipments, should the increase of the city hereafter make such extension necessary.

Guardians, &c., to form one company

Sec. 5. The Guardians, and Assistant Guardians, shall form one Company of Fire Police as aforesaid, consisting of nine sections, and shall be employed to operate Fire Engines, Hose, Hooks, Ladders, Axes, etc., according to the exigencies of the service, and under such Rules and Regulations as may be established by the Fire Committee.

Appointments how made.

Sec. 6. The appointment of the Chief Engineer shall be made by the Council, but the appointment of Assistant Engineer, Guardians, and Assistant Guardians shall be made by the Fire Committee; and the said Fire Committee may at any time suspend or dismiss from the force any of its members (with the exception of the Chief Engineer) who shall be remiss or negligent in the discharge of his duty, or otherwise unfit for the same: Provided, that the power so granted to the Fire Committee of appointing, suspending or dismissing, may be exercised by the Chief Engineer whensoever authorized so to do by the concurrent majority of the said Committee.

Proviso.

Pay of the force.

Sec. 7. The City Council shall fix the compensation to be paid to the Chief Engineer, Assistant Engineer, Hose-maker, Guardians, and Assistant Guardians.

Register to be kept.

Sec. 8. The Chief Engineer shall keep, or cause to be kept, a Register showing the name of every officer and man under his charge in the Depart-, ment, and shall certify the time served, to the Fire Committee, who shall order a warrant or warrants to be drawn on the City Treasurer for the amount due according to the rates fixed by the said Council.

Sec. 9. The City Fire Police shall be sworn as Special Constables, for the purpose of assisting in the maintenance of order in the City, at all times, and more particularly at fires. The Chief of the Fire Department shall have rank in the Police Force as Sub-Chief, the Assistant-Chief as Sergeant, and the men as Sub-Constables. *Fire Police to be sworn as special constables.*

Sec. 10. Any person who shall obstruct any member of the City Fire Police in the performance of his duty as fireman, or shall maliciously cut or in any way injure or damage any portion of the hose, hose reels, fire engines, ladders, or other fire apparatus, shall be liable to a fine not exceeding Twenty Dollars, and costs of prosecution and to an imprisonment not exceeding thirty days for each offence. *Penalty for obstructing firemen.*

Sec. 11. The Stations, and the Dwellings connected therewith, shall be under the immediate control of the Fire Committee, and subject to such orders as they may deem advisable, in the interest of the Department. *Stations, &c., under whose control.*

Sec. 12. The Fire Committee are hereby authorized and required to make and establish such rules and regulations (to be styled " Rules of City Fire Police") for the government of the members of the Fire Department, as may be deemed expedient and proper, to carry out the objects of this by-law. The said rules may prescribe the duties, classification, *Rules and regulations.*

particular service, or distribution of the several officers and men, and may provide penalties and forfeitures, such as suspension from pay, fine, (not to exceed one week's pay) and reprimand, as may be deemed necessary and expedient for the proper regulation of the different portions of the Department.

Ibid.

Sec. 13. All the Rules and Regulations made in pursuance hereof shall be in writing, and fyled in the office of the City Clerk, and shall be binding on all the officers and men connected with the Department after notice thereof. A written or printed copy of such Rules shall be delivered to each member of the Fire Department, and copies shall be posted conspicuously in each Fire Station, and such delivery and posting shall be deemed sufficient notice of the making thereof to the members of the Department.

FIRE ALARMS.

Fire Alarm Telegraph

Sec. 14. Alarms of fire shall be communicated to the Central Office, and from said office to the several Stations, by Electro-Magnetic Telegraph.

Telegraph Operators.

Sec. 15. There shall be one Chief Operator and Superintendent and not less than two Assistant Operators, appointed by the Fire Committee, who shall be charged with the working of the Fire Alarm establishment, under rules and regulations to be fixed and determined by the Fire Committee; the said Chief Operator and Superintendent shall also have charge of the repairs of the Police and Water Department branches; the outlay for such repairs, as well as the proportionate cost of working the said lines. to be chargeable to those respective Departments.

Sec. 16. The compensation to be paid the Chief Operator and Assistant Operators shall be fixed by the City Council. *Their pay.*

Sec. 17. The Chief of Police shall be furnished with keys to open the Alarm Signal Boxes for the use of the officers and Constables of the force, for the purpose of communicating alarms of fire in accordance with such directions as shall be issued from time to time by the Superintendent of the Fire Alarm Telegraph; and it shall be their duty to communicate such alarms whenever they shall have reliable information that a fire has occurred or is in progress. *Policemen to be furnished with keys*

Sec. 18. No person shall open any of the Signal Boxes connected with the City Fire Alarm Telegraph, for the purpose of giving a false alarm, or shall in any way interfere with the said boxes by breaking, cutting, injuring, or defacing the same, or shall turn the cranks therein, except in case of fire, or shall tamper or meddle with the said boxes or shall cut or injure any pole or wire connected with the said Fire Alarm Telegraph, under a Penalty not exceeding Twenty Dollars, and costs of prosecution, and an imprisonment not exceeding Thirty days, for each offence. *Penalty agst. persons interfering with boxes, &c.*

Sec. 19. All the provisions of Article first of By-Law chapter fifteen of the Consolidated By-Lays of the City of Montreal, passed on the tenth day of May, one thousand eight hundred and sixty-five, are hereby repealed.

No. 35.

By-law concerning Firewood.

(Passed 15th March 1870)

Standard cord to consist of.
Sec. 1. The standard cord of Firewood shall be eight feet in length, four feet in height, and three in depth, French measure, from point to scarp, or shall consist of ninety-six cubic feet.

Licensed Corders.
Sec. 2 It shall not be lawful for any person to cord wood for hire unless he shall have first obtained a license from the Inspector of Firewood [hereinafter named], for which he shall pay the sum of One Dollar, which license shall be renewed every year on payment of the same sum. Licensed Corders shall be entitled to receive for the cording of every cord of wood, a sum not exceeding five cents, and shall use approved and stamped measures and no other, and shall allow no crooked limb, or unsound wood to enter into the cord.

Inspector of firewood, his duties.
Sec. 3. The Chief of Police is hereby appointed Inspector of Firewood, and his duties in that capacity shall be to oversee the Corders, and decide cases of dispute, as to the sale, measurement, or delivery of Firewood; he shall also attend at certain fixed hours at his office, to issue licenses, as before ordained, receiving the fees and accounting therefor, monthly to the City Treasurer; he shall keep a register of the number of licenses, the names and residences of the parties receiving them, and shall report for suit, before the Recorder's Court, any cases of misconduct or of infraction of this By-law ;

and the Sub-chiefs and Sergeants of Police are hereby appointed his Deputies, with full power to act in his absence, under his direction.

Sec. 4. It shall not be lawful to sell, in this City, any Firewood in a less quantity than two cords, unless it be measured in a frame duly approved and stamped by the Inspector of Firewood; for doing which he shall receive the sum of twenty-five cents; the said frame to be eight feet long, four feet three inches high, in the clear; and its divisions, if any, to be accordingly. *Firewood in small quantities to be measured in a frame.*

Sec. 5. No Firewood shall be sold in any market or public place in this City except by the cord, or parts of a cord; and any Firewood sold or offered for sale otherwise shall be seized and confiscated by the Inspector of Firewood or Clerk of any market, in the presence of one or more respectable witnesses. *All firewood to be sold by the cord.*

Sec. 6. Nothing herein enacted shall be deemed to have effect as to Firewood the property of Her Majesty's Government. *Government wood excepted.*

Sec. 7. Any person offending against any of the provisions of this By-law shall be liable to a fine not exceeding twenty dollars and costs of prosecution and to an imprisonment not exceeding two months, for each offence. *Penalty*

No. 36.

By-law concerning Offences against good Morals and Decency.

[Passed 15th March 1870.]

Observance of the Lord's day.

Sec. 1. No Merchant, Trader, Petty Chapman, Peddler, Hotel or Tavern-keeper, or any other person keeping a house or place of public entertainment within the limits of the said City, or any other person, shall be allowed to keep open their places of ... , and expose for sale, or be permitted to sell or retail on the Lord's Day, commonly called Sunday, any goods, wares, merchandise, wines, spirits, or other strong or intoxicating liquors; or to purchase or drink the same, in any store, shop, hotel, tavern, house or place of public entertainment, within the limits of the said City.

Taverns to be closed on Sunday.

Sec. 2. No person shall be allowed to open, or keep open any Dram-shop, Tavern, or other place of the same description within the said City, during all the time that will elapse between eleven o'clock in the evening, on each Saturday, and the Monday morning next following.

Gaming, playing cards, &c. prohibited.

Sec. 3. Every description of Gaming, and all Playing of Cards, Dice, or other Games of Chance, with Betting, and all Cock-fighting and Dog-fighting are hereby prohibited and forbidden, in any hotel, restaurant, tavern, inn, or shop, either licenced or unlicensed, in this said City; and any person found guilty of Gaming, or Playing at Cards, or any other Game of Chance, with Betting, in any hotel, restaurant, tavern, inn, or shop, either licensed or unlicensed, in this said City, shall be subject to the penalty hereinafter provided.

Sec. 4. In order the more effectually to repress the offences above specified,—every Police Officer or Constable is hereby authorized to enter each and every shop, hotel, dram-shop, tavern, house, or place of public entertainment within the said City, and to arrest therein, on view, any person or persons found guilty of any of the offences aforesaid. *Police officers authorized to enter houses, &c.*

Sec. 5. No person shall swim or bathe in the River opposite or adjacent to the said City, or the Canal, or other waters adjacent to any of the bridges or avenues leading into the City, so as to be exposed to the view of the inhabitants. *Bathing opposite the City, prohibited.*

Sec. 6. No person shall ill-use or cruelly treat any animal within the said City, either by unnecessarily or mercilessly beating, or by over-loading or over-driving it, or by carrying or transporting it, or by exhibiting or exposing it for sale in an improper manner or one unnecessarily painful, vexatious or dangerous to the said animal, or in any other manner or way whatsoever. *Cruelty to animals.*

Sec. 7. No person shall expose in any of the streets, squares, lanes, highways, or other public places of the said City, any table or device, of any kind whatsoever, upon which any game of chance or hazard can be played; and no person shall play at any such table or device, or unlawful game, in any place as aforesaid. *Tables for gaming upon in the streets prohibited.*

Sec. 8. No person, within the limits of the City of Montreal, shall keep any musical saloon or establishment wherein intoxicating liquors are *Musical saloons prohibited.*

sold, and wherein instrumental music or singing, or both, are used as a means of attracting customers.

Penalty.

Sec. 9. Any person offending against any of the provisions of this By-law shall be liable to a fine not exceeding twenty dollars and costs of prosecution and to an imprisonment not exceeding two months, for each offence.

No. 37.

By-law to Establish a Board of Health in the City of Montreal.

[*Passed* 15*th March* 1870.]

Board of Health established.

Sec. 1. A Board of Health is hereby established and constituted in and for the said City of Montreal.

How constituted.

Sec. 2. The said Board of Health shall consist, at all times, of the Mayor of the City of Montreal for the time being, and of the Members of the Health and Police Committees of the City Council for the time being; and five of them shall at all times constitute a quorum to hold meetings and transact any business relating to public health.

To be increased in case of epdemic.

Sec. 3. Whenever it shall appear that the City of Montreal is threatened with any formidable epidemic, endemic, or contagious disease, it shall be competent to the City Council, by a resolution to that effect passed at any special or quarterly meeting of the Council, to temporarily increase the number of Members of the said Board of Health, and to appoint from time to time, and at all times as aforesaid, an additional number of persons, not less than nine nor exceeding eighteen citizens, inhabitants of the City of Montreal, to be assistant members of the said Board of Health, for a period of time to be expressed in and limited by the resolution appointing them; and during such period such persons so appointed shall, to all intents and purposes, be and remain Members of the said Board, but shall cease to be Members thereof at the expiration of the said period, unless re-appointed.

Sec. 4. The said Board of Health is hereby empowered to adopt and enforce all sanitary measures relating to the cleanliness of the said City; and the said Board and every member thereof shall have power to enter, at all hours in the day time, all Houses, Sheds, Yards, Vacant Lots, and Premises of any kind whatsoever in the said City of Montreal, and order the removal of any offensive matter found therein, and order such cleaning, draining, and purifying as may be deemed necessary for the protection of the public health, and also to enter any Boarding House and Lodging House, and command the removal of persons lodging therein, where the rooms are over-crowded or filthy, or unwholesome, for want of proper ventilation. *Powers of the Board.*

Sec 5. The said Board of Health, during the prevalence of any epidemic, endemic, or contagious disease, shall have also power and authority to prevent the entry into the said City of Montreal of all strangers or emigrants, and all baggage belonging to them, when the appearance of either indicates danger to the public health: to adopt measures *In case of epidemic.*

for purifying, draining, and cleansing of all streets and premises in all ways that may be deemed requisite to preserve the health of the City, and to appoint such Health Officers as may be deemed necessary for superintending or carrying out the orders of the said Board of Health, and to enforce the Rules, Regulations, and By-laws of the Council of the said City of Montreal relative to nuisances : to adopt prompt measures to prevent the spread of any epidemic or contagious disease, when it shall appear by a report of a Physician that any person within the City is afflicted with a disease of that character. To forbid and prevent all communication between any part of the City so infected, except by means of Physicians, Nurses, or Messengers, to carry the necessary advice, medecines, and provisions to the afflicted : to cause any avenue, street, or other passage, to be fenced or enclosed, and to adopt suitable measures for preventing persons from going to, or coming from any part of the City so enclosed : to put itself in communication and in concert with the proper authorities or private institutions and individuals having charge of emigrants on their landing and passage through the Province, the Trinity House, the Harbour Commissioners, and the Board of Works, to establish a place of refuge, or Hospital, in or out of the limits of the City, for poor or sickly emigrants.

Mayor to preside. Sec. 6. The Mayor of the City shall, when present, preside at all meetings of the Board of Health, or, in his absence, the Chairman of the meeting shall be chosen from among the Members of the Health and Police Committees present.

Sec. 7. Whenever from time to time the Statute of the Provincial Parliament, passed in the 12th year of the Reign of Her Majesty Queen Victoria, being chapter the 8th, and intituled "An Act to make provision for the Preservation of the Public Health in certain emergencies." shall, by proclamation of the Governor of the Province, be declared to be in force ; and whilst it shall so continue to be, so as to require the nomination and appointment for the City of Montreal of a Local Board of Health, the Board of Health, hereby constituted shall become and be, and the several and respective Members thereof shall act as "The Local Board of Health for the City of Montreal," and shall carry out and enforce the directions and regulations of the Central Board of Health, and exercise all the powers of Health Officers conferred by that Statute on the Members of the Local Boards of Health. *Local Board of Health.*

Sec. 8. Any person or persons disobeying the orders of the said Board of Health, or of any member of the said Board, or refusing to comply with such orders, or opposing the same in any manner whatsoever, or preventing any Member of the said Board of Health from entering into any house, or on any premises, or assaulting them in the execution of the powers and duties imposed upon them shall be liable to a fine not exceeding twenty dollars and costs of prosecution and to an imprisonment not exceeding two months, for each offence. *Penalty.*

No. 38.

By-law concerning the Sale of Milk.

(Passed, 15th March 1870)

Milk venders to take out license.

Sec. 1. No person shall sell milk in this city unless such person shall have obtained, from the Chief of Police, a license to that effect, for which such person shall pay the sum of one Dollar; which said license shall be renewed every year, on or before the Thirtieth day of May, on payment of a like sum of one Dollar.

Chief of Police to issue licenses.

Register to be kept.

Sec. 2. The Chief of Police is hereby appointed Inspector of milk, and it shall be his duty to see that the provisions of this By-Law are carried out; he shall issue licenses, as before ordained, receiving the fees, and accounting therefor to the City Treasurer; he shall keep a register of the number of licenses, the names and residences of the parties receiving them, and shall report for suit, before the Recorder's Court, any cases of infraction of this By-Law; and the sub-Chiefs and sergeants of Police are hereby appointed his deputies, for the purposes of this By-Law, with full power to act in his absence.

Measures to be stamped.

Sec. 3. All measures, cans or other vessels used in the sale of milk shall be stamped according to law.

Adulterated Milk prohibited.

Sec. 4. No person shall sell milk produced from cows fed upon any substance deleterious to the quality of milk, nor shall any person adulterate by water or otherwise, milk to be sold in this City, or sell or cause to be sold in the said city adulterated, unwholesome or diluted milk; and any person in the employment of another, who shall knowingly violate any provision of this section, shall be held equally guilty with the principal, and suffer the same penalty or punishment.

Sec. 5. The Chief of Police or his deputies, as aforesaid, may, and they are hereby authorised, to enter any place or premises where milk is stored or kept for sale, and to stop and inspect all vehicles used in the conveyance of milk, and whenever they have reason to believe any milk found therein is adulterated, they shall take specimens thereof and cause the same to be analysed or otherwise satisfactorily tested, and they shall preserve a certificate of the result of said analysis or test, sworn to by the analyser or tester, to serve as evidence in the prosecution. *Police authorized to enter premises, &c.*

Sec. 6. It shall be the duty of the Inspector of Milk to cause the name and place of business of all persons convicted under the preceding Section to be published in the newspapers in which the advertisements of the Corporation of the said City usually appear. *Names of parties violating this By-Law to be published.*

Sec. 7. Any person offending against any of the provisions of this By-law shall be liable to a fine not exceeding twenty dollars and costs of prosecution and to an imprisonment not exceeding two months, for each offence. *Penalty.*

No. 39.

By-law concerning Nuisances.

(Passed 15th March 1870)

Vacant lots to be enclosed.
SEC. 1. Every lot of land whereon no building is erected, on the line of any public street or lane in this City, shall be, on the line of such street, enclosed with a stone or brick wall, or with a wooden fence, at least six feet, French mesure, in height, above the level and on the line of such street, as fixed and determined by the City Surveyor, with posts properly put up, so that the said fence shall not lean over or encroach upon the said street or lane.

After fifteen days notice.
SEC. 2. Every proprietor of such vacant lot of land, or his agent, or the person having or assuming the care of such lot of land, or any occupant thereof shall be bound to make and erect, or cause to be made and erected, such wall or fence within fifteen days after such proprietor, agent or occupant shall have been notified so to do by the City Surveyor or his Deputy, under the penalty of a fine not exceeding twenty dollars and costs of prosecution and an imprisonment not exceeding two months, for each offence.

City Surveyor to fence in lot in certain cases.
SEC. 3. It shall be the duty of the City Surveyor, if such lot of land be not enclosed, as above stated, within the delay hereinbefore fixed, or in case the proprietor thereof can not be found, to cause the said lot to be enclosed with a wooden fence at the cost

and charge of the proprietor or the person having or assuming the care thereof.

SEC. 4. Whenever there shall be on any lot of land in the said City of Montreal stagnant or putrid water, or any filthy, infected or putrid matter, or the said lot shall be offensive or dangerous to the public health, it shall be the duty as well of the occupant as of the proprietor of the said lot, or the agent of the proprietor thereof, or of any person having or assuming the charge thereof, to fill up, level or drain the same, as the case may be, or to remove the offensive, infected or putrid matters thereon, without the necessity of a notice to that effect; and any such proprietor, agent, occupant or person having the charge of the said lot, who shall neglect during two days to remove and abate such nuisance shall be liable to a fine not exceeding twenty dollars and costs of prosecution and to an imprisonment not exceeding two months, for each offence. *Lots having stagnant water, &c., to be drained.*

SEC. 5. It shall be the duty of the City Surveyor after the expiration of the delay prescribed for the removal or abatement of such nuisance, to cause to be done on the said lot of land, at the cost and charge of the proprietor, or the person having or assuming the charge of the said lot, whatever may be necessary for removing or otherwise abating the said nuisance, either by causing drains to be made thereon or by filling up the said lot, or by removing or otherwise abating the offensive, infected or putrid matters. *City surveyor duty if nuisance be not abated.*

SEC. 6. No person shall, in any manner, carry, convey, deposit or place, or cause to be carried, conveyed, deposited or placed into, or upon, any pre- *Penalty for depositing nuisances.*

mises, or lot of land, in this City, or into, or upon, any public square, street, lane or other place whatsoever in this City, any dead carcass, ordure, filth, dirt, dust, or any offensive matter or substance whatever; and no person shall commit any nuisance, or cause or permit any such to be committed, into, or upon, any such premises or lot of land, public square, street, lane, or other place whatsoever in this City, under the penalty of a fine not exceeding twenty dollars and costs of prosecution and to an imprisonment not exceeding two months, for each offence: Provided that nothing herein contained shall prevent the deposit of dust, rubbish, and the sweepings of streets and yards in those places within the said City, specially set apart by the Council for that purpose.

In carting filth, none to be dropped in street.

SEC. 7. In carting, carrying, or conveying any ordure, filth, dirt, dust, or any offensive matter or substance whatsoever, through any public square, street or lane, no part thereof shall be allowed to drop or fall from the vehicle carting, carrying or conveying the same; and for every offence against the provisions hereof, the owner of the said vehicle, as well as the driver or person in charge thereof, shall be liable to a Fine not exceeding Twenty Dollars and costs of prosecution and to an imprisonment not exceeding two months, for each offence.

Offensive premises.

SEC. 8. If any person shall own, occupy or keep any lot of ground or other premises in such bad and filthy condition as to be offensive and a nuisance to the neighborhood or to any person or family, such person shall be subject to a Fine not exceeding twenty dollars and cost of prosecution and to an im-

prisonment not exceeding two months, for each of- *Penalty.*
fence.

SEC. 9. Any soap boiler, chandler, butcher, or *Putrid substances.*
other person who shall keep, or collect, or cause to
be kept or collected, any stale, putrid or stinking
fat, grease or other matter, shall for each offence, be
liable to a fine not exceeding twenty dollars and *Penalty.*
costs of prosecution, and in default of immediate
payment of the said fine and costs, the defendant
may be imprisoned in the common goal for a period
not exceeding two months, the said imprisonment
to cease upon payment of the said fine and costs.

SEC. 10. Any owner or occupant of any tallow *Soap factories, tallow chandleries, &c*
chandler's shop, soap factory, tannery, slaughter
house, stable, or grocery, who shall suffer such establishments or premises to become nauseous, foul or
offensive, shall be liable to a fine not exceeding
twenty dollars and costs of prosecution and to an
imprisonment not exceeding two months, for each
offence.

SEC. 11. Every occupant of a house in the said *Yards to be kept clean.*
City, shall keep the yard or premises therewith
connected, in a clean state, and free from filth or
offensive substances, and shall collect in one place,
in such yard or yards, all the house dirt or offal, under a Penalty not exceeding Five Dollars and costs
of prosecution for each offence: Provided that when
the accumulation of such dirt or offal shall be equal
to a load, or become offensive, it shall be removed,
under a like penalty.

Sec 12. The occupant of any house or building *Dirty water from premises.*
in the said City, who shall permit or cause to be

discharged, by any channel or gutter, or in any other way whatsoever, from such house or building, into any street, square, lane, or highway, in the said City, any dirty or stinking water, or any thing that may cause public inconvenience or annoyance, shall for each offence, be liable to a fine not exceeding twenty dollars and costs of prosecution, and in default of immediate payment of the said fine and costs, the defendant may be imprisoned in the common goal for a period not exceeding two months, the said imprisonment to cease upon payment of the said fine and costs.

Ditto thrown into street. Sec. 13. Any occupant of any house or building in the said City, who shall throw, or permit to be thrown, any dirty water, ashes, soot, snow, or ice, or any sweepings, rubbish, dirt or filth whatsoever, into any square, street, lane, or highway, in the said City, shall be liable to a fine not exceeding twenty dollars and costs of prosecution and to an imprisonment not exceeding two months, for each offence.

Swine, &c. Sec. 14. Any person who shall keep any swine, dogs, foxes, or other such animals on their premises, in the said City, shall maintain the houses, buildings, or pens in which the same shall be kept in such a clean state that the neighbours and passengers may not be incommoded by the smell therefrom, under a Penalty not exceeding twenty Dollars and cost of prosecution, for each offence.

Dead animals Sec. 15. The owner of every animal that shall die or be found dead in any of the streets, squares, lanes, highways, or on any enclosed or unenclosed ground in the said City, shall immediately cause such animal to be buried, at least three feet below the surface of the earth, under a penalty not exceeding twenty dollars and costs of prosecution for each offence: and any person who shall throw any such dead animal into any ditch, pond, canal, or stream or sewer, or in the river opposite the said City, shall be liable to a fine not exceeding twenty dollars and costs of prosecution and to an imprisonment not exceeding two months, for each offence, and whenever the owner of such animal, or the person committing the offence aforesaid, cannot be discovered, it shall be the duty of the Police Officer of the district to cause the removal of such nuisance.

Sec. 16. It shall be the duty of the Chief Police, and of the officers and men under his command, to enforce or cause to be enforced, all the provisions of this By-law; and for that purpose the said Chief of Police, and the said officers and men of the Police Force are hereby severally and collectively authorized to visit and examine any house, lot, premises, or building in this City; and any person who shall obstruct, hinder or oppose them, or any of them in the discharge of such duty, shall be liable to a fine not exceeding twenty dollars and costs of prosecution and to an imprisonment not exceeding two months, for each offence. *[margin: Police officers to enforce this By-Law. Authority to visit premises. Penalty.]*

No. 40.

By-law concerning Sinks, Privies and Cess-Pools.

(Passed 15th March, 1870)

Sec. 1. The owner, agent, occupant, or other person, having the care of any tenement used as a *[margin: Privies to be connected with drains.]*

dwelling house, or of any other building with which there is a privy connected and used, shall furnish the same with a sufficient drain of glazed earthen tile under ground, to carry off the waste water, and also with a suitable privy or water closet : the privy vault shall be sunk in the ground and built in the manner hereinafter prescribed, and of a capacity proportionate to the number of inhabitants of such tenement or those having occasion to use such privy : provided always that in case no sewer exists in the street, then no drain from the cess-pool or privy shall be required.

Privies. How constructed. Sec. 2. All vaults and privies shall be constructed so that the inside of the same shall be four feet from the line of the adjoining lot. Every Privy-vault shall be made tight, so that the contents shall not escape therefrom.

In case tenements are unprovided with privies. Sec. 3. If the Chief of Police or other officer appointed for this purpose by the Board of Health shall at any time be satisfied that any tenement used as a dwelling house, or any other building, as mentioned in the first section, is not provided with a suitable privy, vault and drain, or either of them as aforesaid, the said Chief of Police, or other officer may give notice in writing, to the owner, agent or person having the care thereof, or in case the owner, agent, or person having the care thereof is unknown or absent from the City, give public notice in one English and one French newspaper printed in this City, requiring such owner, agent, occupant, or other person, within such time as the said Chief of Police or other officer as aforesaid, shall appoint, to cause a proper and sufficient privy, vault and drain, or either of them, to be constructed for such tenement or other building; and in case of neglect or refusal to obey such notice, the Chief of Police, or other officer appointed for this purpose by the Board of Health, shall have power to cause such privy, vault and drain to be made for such tenement or other building, the expense of which shall be paid by such owner, agent, occupant, or other person; and in case such drain, vault and privy are constructed as aforesaid for the use of more than one house, then the owner, agent, occupant or other person having the charge of each such house shall be liable to pay a proportionate part of such expense.

Sec. 4. Whenever any vault, privy or drain shall become offensive or obstructed, the owner, occupant, agent or other person having charge of the land on which any such vault, privy or drain may be situated, shall remove, cleanse, alter, amend or repair the same within such reasonable time after notice in writing to that effect given by the Chief of Police, or his deputy, as shall be expressed in such notice. In case of neglect or refusal so to do, the Chief of Police, or other officer appointed for this purpose by the Board of Health, shall cause the same to be removed, altered, amended, or repaired as he may deem fit, at the expense of the owner, agent, occupant or other person as aforesaid. *Privies. When offensive, &c.*

Sec. 5. No vault or privy shall be emptied between the first day of June and the fifteenth day of September in each year, unless, on inspection caused to be made, the Chief of Police, or other officer appointed for this purpose by the Board of Health, shall be satisfied of the necessity of the same, for the *Time fixed for emptying privies.*

health of the inhabitants. In such case no more of the contents shall be taken away than they or either of them shall deem to be absolutely necessary for present safety and relief, and such precautions shall be used for the prevention of any offensive effluvia, as they or either of them shall direct, at the expense of the owner, agent, occupant or other person having charge of the premises.

Books to be kept at Police Stations for applications, &c.

Sec. 6. Books shall be kept at each Police Station under the charge of the head officer thereof, in which shall be entered all applications for opening and cleansing vaults; and the same shall receive attention in the several wards in the order in which they are made. All Vaults and Privies requiring cleansing shall be emptied between the first day of October and the first day of May in each year; if not cleaned within the aforesaid dates, the occupant or owner of the premises on which such vaults and privies are situated, shall pay a fine not exceeding ten dollars for neglecting to clean the same; and in every such case the officer appointed by the Board of Health shall order the immediate cleansing of the said vaults and privies, the expense whereof shall be charged to and paid by the owner or occupant in default as aforesaid. The Board of Health shall fix a tariff of charges for services under this By-law.

Tariff of charges.

Chief of Police to license night scavengers.

Sec. 7. The Chief of Police is hereby authorised to grant licenses to night Scavengers applying for the same, for which each applicant shall pay the sum of two Dollars; which said licenses shall be renewed every year, on or before the thirtieth day of May, on payment of a like sum of two dollars.

Sec. 8. The night Scavengers who may be licensed shall be governed by the regulations which may from time to time be made by the Board of Health. Charges for cleansing vaults and privies, under the provisions of this By-law, shall be paid to the Contractor according to such tariff as may be authorised by the said Board of Health. *Regulations for night scavengers.*

Sec. 9. All waste water shall be conveyed through sufficient drains underground to a common sewer, where one exists, in the street. *Waste water.*

Sec. 10. Each Scavenger shall be provided with a tight vehicle of approved pattern which shall be completely covered in on all sides and at top and shall have the number of his license, and also the number of cubic yards which such vehicle is capable of conveying, painted in black figures on a white ground, the figures to be at least four inches in size. And all such vehicles shall be of the same size and capacity, and the Chief of Police shall Register the number of each licensed vehicle and its capacity in cubic yards. *Scavengers to use light vehicles, &c.*

Sec. 11. It shall be the duty of such Night Scavengers, when notified, to clean and remove the contents of vaults, and to deposit the same, where directed by the Chief of Police, and they shall dispose of the said contents so that no offensive effluvia shall arise therefrom. *Duties of scavengers defined.*

Sec. 12. No person shall cover over any sink or privy that may be full, nor draw off the contents thereof into any hole or place dug or made to receive the same. And the Chief of Police shall cause such matter so buried as aforesaid to be dug up and *Privies, when full not to be covered over, &c.*

carried away at the cost of the person so burying the same.

Duties of scavengers further defined. Sec. 13. It shall be the duty of the Licensed Scavenger for each District to visit, at least once in each year, all the privies within his District. He shall have, for this purpose, the right of entry to private premises between the hours of seven in the morning and six in the afternoon daily—Sundays and holidays excepted—and he shall report to the Police any vaults or privies found in contravention of this By-law, and the officer appointed for this purpose shall, after ascertaining the correctness of such report, take the necessary action to have the same cleansed as aforesaid, or made to conform to this By-law.

Tariff of charges. Sec. 14. The Night Scavengers shall be paid at the rate of so much per cubic foot, of contents of any such vault, or at the rate of so much per load.

Sec. 15. No person other than a duly licensed night scavenger shall engage in such business or perform such duty.

Duties of scavengers. Sec. 16. The night scavengers having undertaken a work shall complete the same with all possible dispatch, and shall make good all damage to any such Privy or Vault whilst cleaning the same, and shall, when the work is completed, restore the same to the condition it was in before the work was commenced.

Penalty. Sec. 17. Any person violating any of the provisions of this By-law, shall, for each offence, be liable to a fine not exceeding twenty dollars and costs of prosecution, and in default of immediate payment of the said fine and costs, the defendant may be im-

language, in which the notices of the Council usually appear, which notice shall also be placarded on the front of the building or premises in which such engine or factory is to be used or established as aforesaid; and no application for leave to erect or use any steam-engine, factory or establishment of any of the kinds mentioned in the foregoing section, shall or may be received by the said Council, unless notice thereof shall have been given in the said newspapers, and placarded as aforesaid at least ten days before the time of making the said application, so that residents in the vicinity of the applicant, or the place where it is intended to erect, use or employ the said engine, factory or establishment, and others interested, may be afforded an opportunity to oppose the granting of the said application, and time, if necessary, to be heard upon their opposition.

Sec. 4 Upon the receipt of any application for leave to erect, use or employ any steam-engine, factory or establishment of any of the kinds hereinbefore enumerated, the Inspector of Buildings shall proceed to inspect the premises wherein it is intended to erect, use or employ the said engine, factory or establishment, and shall certify in writing whether the said premises and the apparatus connected therewith, are in conformity with the law, and so made as not to endanger the surrounding property, or affect the public health or safety : a copy of which certificate shall be delivered to the applicant and another to the Fire Committee ; and for such inspection and certificate, the said Inspector is hereby authorized to ask and demand from each

Premises to be inspected, &c.

applicant as aforesaid, for and on behalf of the Corporation of this City, the sum of two dollars.

Petroleum, coal oil, &c.

Sec. 5. No person shall have, keep, sell, or manufacture in any place or building within the limits of the City of Montreal, any crude or refined petroleum, earth or rock oil, benzole, benzine, naphtha, kerosene, coal oil or burning fluid, in larger quantity than five barrels in the aggregate, except it be kept in close iron tanks, or in *detached* and properly ventilated stores or buildings specially adapted for that purpose, by having raised sills or other contrivances, so as effectually to prevent the overflow of such substances beyond the premises where the same are kept or stored.

Storage of do.

Sec. 6. No person shall manufacture or store any of the articles mentioned in the next preceding section, in any wooden building, or any wooden building encased with brick, or any building covered with shingles or other wooden material, within the limits of the City, except when such articles shall be secured in suitable iron tanks.

Same.

Sec. 7. No person shall manufacture or store any of the articles mentioned in the fifth section, in any larger quantity than is specified in the said section, in any building situate less than one hundred feet from any other building, and unless separated from said building by a brick or stone wall not less than ten feet in height.

Same.

Sec. 8. It shall not be necessary that such building shall be enclosed by a wall as provided in the preceding section in any case where it shall be not less than three hundred feet from any other building, and provided also that none of the articles enumerated in said fifth section shall be stored or kept above the ground story of said building. Provided, also, that in no case shall buildings used for such storage be connected with any adjoining store or building by drains or sewers of any kind.

Sec. 9. Every person desiring to manufacture, keep or store, any of the articles mentioned in section fifth of this By-law, in any quantity exceeding five barrels, as hereinbefore specified, shall make written application therefor to the Fire Committee, stating in said application the place or building in which he desires to manufacture, sell, or store, said articles, and the manner in which he proposes to keep them; and it shall be the duty of the Inspector of Buildings, or in his absence, the Chief Engineer of the Fire Department, to examine the premises and report to the Fire Committee, whether in his opinion said premises are made conformable to the provisions of this By-law; and upon his report the said Fire Committee shall take action and grant or refuse the license, as to them may seem meet, subject, however, to the approval of the said Council. *License for storage of do.*

Sec. 10. All licenses granted under the provisions of the preceding section, shall continue and be in force from the time of granting the same until the first day of May next ensuing, and shall be renewed every year on payment of the fee hereinafter provided. *Term of said license.*

Sec. 11. Every person at the time of receiving said license, shall pay the sum of two dollars to be accounted for to the City Treasurer. *Fee.*

162 BY-LAWS.

Premises to be examined. Sec. 12. It shall be the duty of the Inspector of buildings, or in his absence or inability, it shall be the duty of the Chief Engineer of the Fire Department in addition to the duties already severally imposed upon them by law, to examine all premises where either of the said articles mentioned in section fifth are manufactured, kept, or stored, so as to insure a strict compliance with the foregoing provisions, and they or either of them shall immediately prosecute all offenders against any of the provisions of this by-law.

Steam engines, how heated. Sec. 13. No steam-engine in this City shall hereafter be heated with wood, or with any other description of fuel than coal, from the first day of May to the first day of November, inclusive, in each year, unless the funnel or chimney thereof be covered with a wire netting or cap, sufficient to prevent the escape or emission of sparks of fire therefrom.

Boilers for soap, &c. Sec. 14. Every kettle, boiler, or copper, for the use of any tallow-chandler, soap-boiler, painter, chemist, druggist, or other such artificer, within the said City shall be so fixed or erected in brick or stone, laid in mortar, and grouted with liquid mortar so as to prevent all communication between the contents of such kettle, boiler, or copper and the fire; and the fire place under every such kettle, boiler, or copper shall be so constructed and secured, by an iron door, as to enclose the fire therein.

Hot-air furnaces. Sec. 15. No person shall hereafter build, construct or erect any Hot-Air Furnace, or cause the same to be built, constructed or erected, in any house or premises in this City, except in the manner hereinafter provided.

Sec. 16. The only manner in which it shall be permitted for any person hereafter to build, construct, or erect, any Hot-Air Furnace in any house or premises in this City, or to cause the same to be built, constructed or erected therein, shall be as follows, viz. : {How constructed.}

First.—In all cases when the Hot-Air Chamber in which the furnace is to be placed, shall be made of brick, it must be built on a stone foundation, and of at least eight-inch brick work, well laid in mortar, and arched over the top with eight-inch work, with a lining of tin inside the arch; in which said lining of tin the warm air tubes must be properly riveted, and they must also be made to pass through the arch; the said arch to be surrounded with an iron band four inches by one quarter inch, to keep the said brick-work together. {Hot-air chamber.}

Second.—A space of at least twelve inches must be left between the upper surface of the warm-air chamber and the bottom of the beams or ceiling; the said beams or ceiling must be covered with a sheet of bright tin plate secured thereto, seamed or soldered together, which must extend six inches beyond the top of the furnace on three sides, and one foot six inches on the front, above the furnace door. {Same.}

Third.—When portable furnaces are to be used, they must be placed on a cast iron pan or stand, said pan or stand to be placed upon a layer of bricks, tiles, or other non-combustible material (if on a {Portable furnaces} wooden floor); the said pan or stand to project three inches beyond the hot air sheeting. And if the said furnace-top be within two feet of the ceiling or beams, then the said ceiling or beams must be protected in the same manner as in the brick furnace, as mentioned above.

Smoke-pipe.   *Fourth.*—The smoke pipe must be made of, at least, No. 20 sheet Iron, and of a size proportionate to the furnace, and provided with a key or damper to check the draft; the said pipe must be properly joined; must be nine inches from any wood-work, and must be conducted into a proper chimney.

Warm-air tubes.   *Fifth.*—The warm air tubes from the top of the furnace under the first floor, must be made of bright tin, and must not pass nearer than four inches to any wood-work, and be enclosed with solid brick work, or said hot air tubes shall consist of double tubes made of tin plate riveted together at the joints the space between them to be filled up with plaster of Paris.

Hot-air registers.   *Sixth.*—All hot air registers hereafter placed in the floor of any dwelling, store, church or other building, shall be set in soap stone borders of the following dimensions, to wit: Registers smaller than twelve inches long by nineteen inches wide, shall have a soap stone border not less than three inches in width and one and a quarter inches in thickness. All registers twelve by nineteen and less than fifteen by twenty-five inches, shall have a border not less than five inches wide and one and a half inches in thickness; and all registers fifteen by twenty-five inches or more shall have a border not less than six inches wide and two inches in thickness. All soap stone borders to be firmly set in plaster of Paris or gauged mortar; all register boxes to be double and to be made of tin plate with a flange on the top to fit the groove in the soap stone. There shall also be an open space of two inches on all sides of the register box extending from the under side of the ceiling below the register to the soap stone in the floor; the outside of said space to be covered with a casing of tin plate made tight on all sides, to extend from the underside of the aforesaid ceiling up to and turn under the said soap stone. Registers twelve by nineteen inches, or less than fifteen by twenty five inches, shall have a space of three inches between the register box and casing; registers of fifteen by twenty-five and more shall have a space of three and a half inches. All horizontal registers must have a diaphragm of wire cloth so placed as to prevent any combustible from entering the hot air tubes. All the openings through the base or skirting must have a stone frame or double tin filled with plaster of Paris one inch in thickness through all the wood work into the brick or other conductor.

Seventh.—The cold air conductor must be of cast iron, strong sheet iron or brick, for, at least, three feet from the hot-air chamber; the remainder of it may be of wood, provided a wire screen be properly secured between the said iron or brick, and wood; and no gas pipe must be allowed to pass nearer than one foot six inches from any smoke-pipe or hot-air conductor. Cold-air conductor.

Eighth.—No high pressure steam pipe shall be laid or placed in contact with any wood between Steam-pipes.

floors and ceilings, or in plastered walls or partitions. When such steam pipes are used for heating, they shall be placed or inclosed in sand, brick, mortar, or other incombustible substance.

Furnaces to be inspected, &c.

Sec. 17. No person or persons shall use or put in operation, or cause to be used, or put in operation, any hot-air furnace, that may hereafter be built, constructed, or erected, in any house or premises in this City, until the same shall have been first inspected and examined by the Inspector of Buildings, and until the said Inspector shall have furnished a certificate that the same is built, constructed, or erected in the manner hereinbefore provided.

Fee.

Sec. 18. The said Inspector of Buildings is hereby authorized to ask and demand, for and on behalf of the Corporation of this City, a fee of four dollars, for each and every such examination and certificate made and furnished by him as aforesaid.

Stove-pipes.

Sec. 19. No person shall hereafter pass, or cause to be passed through any partition of wood, or wood and lime, or through a wooden floor where there is no pipe-stone or iron pipe having flanges, one of which shall rest upon the floor, and the other connect with the ceiling under said floor, and having said iron pipe surrounded with brick work, in any house or building within the said City, any Stove-pipe, without leaving six inches clear between the pipe and such partition or floor.

Pipe-holes not to be left open.

Sec. 20. No occupant or occupants of any house or building within the said City, shall permit any Pipe-hole not in use in any chimney in such house or building to remain open, and not closed with a stopper of metal or other incombustible material.

Sec. 21. No person shall hereafter manufacture any kind of Fireworks, or Friction Matches, in any house or building in the said City, without a written permission or certificate from the said Inspector, for which he shall be entitled to demand and receive the sum of Two Dollars for the said Corporation; Provided, that no such permission or certificate shall be granted when such house or building shall adjoin or be in the immediate vicinity of other buildings. *Friction matches.*

Sec. 22. All persons in this City having Lucifer Matches, or Matches capable of being ignited by friction, in their possession, whether for use or sale, shall keep the same in stone, brick, or metal safes or boxes. *To be kept in safes.*

Sec. 23. No person shall keep, connected with or lying upon wood, any Unslacked Lime, in any House, Outhouse, or Wooden Building within the said City; or shall keep, or permit to be kept any loose Straw or Hay in any house in which he, she, or they shall live; or shall set fire to or burn any Shavings, Chips, Straw, or other combustible materials, for the sole purpose of consuming the same, in any street, square, or lane in the said City, or within any enclosure, within one hundred and fifty feet of any building, or shall carry, or keep, or suffer to be carried or kept, any lighted candle or lamp, in any livery or other stable in the said City, unless such lamp or candle shall be so enclosed in a lantern or shade as to prevent any accidents by fire therefrom. *Unslacked lime.* *Shavings, &c.* *Lamps in stables.*

Smoking in stables, &c.

Sec. 24. No person shall smoke, or have in his possession any lighted pipe or cigar in any Rope-walk, Stable, Barn, Carpenter's or Cabinet-maker's Work-shop, or other shop or building where straw, shavings, or other such combustible materials may be, or shall carry fire through any of the streets, squares, lanes, or court-yards in the said City, except in some covered metal vessel or fire-pan.

Storage of ashes.

Sec. 25. All Ash-holes, or Ash-houses for the keeping or storage of Ashes within the said City, shall be built of stone, brick, or iron, without the use of wood in any part thereof.

Same.

Sec. 26. No person shall place or keep any Wood-ashes, removed from stoves or fire-places, in any wooden box, or near any wooden partition in his, her, or their house or houses, in the said City, or in any out-house or shed; or shall place, or permit to be placed, any Hay, Straw, or other combustible materials, uncovered, in his or their yard or court-yard, or any lot of ground within one hundred feet of any building.

Woodyards.

Sec. 27. No person shall hereafter keep for sale or storage any Cord Wood or other Wood, Boards, Planks, or other wooden building materials, in any Yard in the said City, so near neighbouring buildings as to endanger the same, should fire occur, or shall keep such Yard without having the same inspected by the said Inspector, and without having received from him a Certificate of Inspection; for which certificate the said Inspector shall be entitled to demand and receive the sum of one dollar, for and on account of the said Corporation.

Sec. 28. It shall not be lawful for any person or persons to keep or sell any *Fireworks* within the limits of this City in any quantity without first having obtained from the Inspector of buildings a license therefor, on which shall be written or printed a copy of Rules and Regulations, relative to the keeping and storage of Fireworks within the said City; and every such license shall be in force until the first day of May next ensuing the date thereof, unless sooner annulled by said Inspector, and no longer; but such license may, prior to the expiration of that term, be renewed from year to year by endorsement thereon: provided always that such license may be rescinded at any time by the said Inspector, should the holder thereof have infringed the aforesaid Rules and Regulations. <small>Fireworks.</small>

Sec. 29. The Inspector of Buildings shall be entitled to demand and receive a fee of One dollar, to be paid to the City Treasurer, for every such license and renewal of license for the keeping, selling and storing of Fireworks within the limits of this City. <small>Fee.</small>

Sec. 30. No person shall fire or discharge any gun, fowling-piece, firearms, or shall set fire to any cracker, squib, serpent, or rocket, or shall throw any lighted cracker, squib, serpent or rocket in any of the streets, squares, or lanes of the said City, or nearer than eighty yards to any house or building within the limits of the same. <small>Discharge of firearms and fireworks prohibited.</small>

Sec. 31. Each Chimney and flue thereof in use in the City of Montreal. shall hereafter be required to be swept by a licensed sweep or sweeps of the said City, three times in the course of each and every <small>Chimneys, how to be swept.</small>

twelve months, beginning on, and to be computed from the first day of the month of May in each and every year, namely: Once between the first day of the month of May and the first day of the month of November in each and every year, and twice at intervals of at least two months, time from each other, between the said first day of the month of November and first day of the following month of May.

Chief of Police to license sweepers.

Sec. 32. It shall be lawful for the Chief of Police to annually issue and grant licenses to sweep the Chimneys and flues thereof, throughout the said City to so many persons of honest character and steady habits as he may deem expedient and necessary; and to revoke and withdraw the said licenses whensoever and as often as occasion may require, or the dishonesty of character, or impropriety of conduct, of the person or persons to whom the same may have been granted, shall justify the same being done. Provided, however, that no licensed sweep shall use any brush, broom, or other contrivance for the purpose of sweeping Chimneys without first having submitted the same to the Inspector of Buildings for his approval.

Fee.

Sec. 33. Each and every person receiving any such license, shall pay the City Treasurer therefor, through the Chief of Police, at and after the following rates, viz:

For the license of a Master Sweeper, granted to himself, the sum of Five Dollars.

For the license of each and every man or boy employed by him, the sum of One Dollar.

Sec. 34. All licensed sweepers shall be under the superintendence of the Inspector of Buildings, and it shall be their duty to obey all orders and instructions of the said Inspector, relating to the sweeping of Chimneys. *Sweepers—under whose superintendence.*

Sec. 35. The following shall be and the same is hereby established as the only tariff or rates of fees to be allowed and exacted, by each and every licensed sweep or sweeps, for thoroughly cleansing and sweeping the Chimneys and flues thereof in the said City, viz: *Tariff of charges.*

For sweeping each Chimney or flue thereof in a one-story house, Five Cents.

For sweeping each Chimney or flue thereof in a two-story house, Eight Cents.

For sweeping each Chimney or flue thereof in a three-story house, Ten Cents.

For sweeping each Chimney or flue thereof in a house of four or more stories, Twelve and a half Cents.

Sec. 36. Whenever any flue or Chimney within the said City shall take fire, and it shall appear that the occupier or occupiers of the house or building where such flue or Chimney may be, had refused or neglected to have the same swept at the periods hereinbefore specified, every such occupier or occupiers shall be liable to the penalty hereinafter provided. *Penalty for flue taking fire.*

Sec. 37. The Chief Engineer of the Fire Department, or in his absence or disability, the Assistant Engineer, shall have power to direct the pulling down or demolishing of any house or building *Power to pull down building at fires.*

Proviso. which he shall judge necessary to be so pulled down or demolished in order to prevent the spreading of fire. Provided however that he shall have first obtained the sanction of the Mayor for the time being, or in his absence, that of the Acting Mayor or the Chairman of the fire Committee, for so doing.

Penalty. Sec. 38. Any person offending against any of the provisions of this Bylaw shall be liable to a fine not exceeding twenty dollars and costs of prosecution and to an imprisonment not exceeding two months, for each offence.

No. 42.

By-law to Preserve Public Peace and Good Order.

[Passed 15th March 1870.]

Riots, &c., prohibited. Sec. 1. All riots, noises, disturbances, or disorderly assemblages, are hereby prohibited in this City; and all persons making or creating any riot, noise, disorder, or disturbance, or forming part of any disorderly assemblage anywhere within the limits of the said City, shall incur the Penalty hereinafter provided.

Religious worship not to be molested. Sec. 2. No person shall disquiet or disturb any Congregation or assembly met for religious worship, by making a noise or by rude and indecent behaviour, or profane discourse within their place of worship, or so near the same as to disturb the order and solemnity of the meeting.

False alarms of fire, &c. Sec 3. No person shall wilfully give or make a false alarm of fire or watch, or shall employ any

Bellman, or use or cause to be used any bell, horn, or bugle, or other sounding instrument (save and except at any religious or military ceremony or procession); or shall employ any device, noise or performance tending in either case, to the collection of persons on the streets, sidewalks, or other public places, to the obstruction of the same, for any purpose whatsoever, without permission of the Mayor in writing.

Sec. 4. Any person offending against any of the provisions of this By-law shall be liable to a fine not exceeding twenty dollars and costs of prosecution and to an imprisonment not exceeding two months, for each offence. _{Penalty.}

No. 43.

By-law concerning Public Pounds.

(Passed 15th March 1870.)

Sec. 1. No Horse, Cattle, Swine, Hog, Sheep, or Goat, shall be permitted to run a large at any time in the City, or graze, browse, or feed upon any of of the streets, squares, lanes, alleys, or public places of this City, under the following Penalties against the owners or keepers, or persons having charge of the same, viz: _{No horse, cattle &c. to run at large}

For each Stallion, Bull, Boar, or Ram $1 00 _{Penalty}
  "   Hog or Swine..................... 0 50
  "   Gelding, Mare, Ox, or Cow... 0 25
  "   Colt, Filly, Calf or Goat...... 0 20
  "   Sheep.................................. 0 10

Public pounds established.

Sec. 2. Public Pounds shall be, and they are hereby established in this City, as follows, viz: one at the Cattle Market, in the St. James' Ward; one at the St, St. Gabriel Market, in the St. Ann's Ward, of the said City, and one at each of the Police Stations in the said City; and the Clerks of the said Markets, for the time being, and the Sergeants or Policemen, on duty at the said Stations, shall have charge and act as Keepers of the said Pounds respectively.

Impounding animals.

Sec. 3. All Horses, Cattle, Swine, Hogs, Sheep, or Goats found at large within the said City, or grazing, browsing, or feeding upon any of the streets, squares, lanes, or alleys of the said City, may be taken by any person or persons and driven or carried to either of the said pounds, or to any Police Station in the said City, for delivery at the nearest Pound;

Duties of pound keepers.

and it shall be the duty of the Pound-keepers, or persons having charge of such Pounds, to receive and impound the same, and to enter in a book to be kept by them for that purpose, the names and places of abode of all persons who may bring any such horse, cattle, swine, hog, sheep, or goat to such Pounds, and the time of bringing the same respectively; and the said Pound-keepers shall pay to the persons bringing any such horse, cattle, swine, hog, sheep, or goat to such Pounds, one half of the penalty incurred for each and every animal as hereinbefore provided.

Duty of policemen.

Sec. 4. It shall be the duty of all Constables of the Police Force of the said City, whenever they see or meet any horse, cattle, swine, hog, sheep, or goat, running at large in contravention of this By-law, or

whenever their attention is directed by any Citi-
..en to any such animal running at large as aforesaid
to immediately drive the same to the nearest Pound.

Sec. 5. If the owner of any such horse, swine, hog, sheep, or goat, or any other person entitled to redeem the same, shall appear and claim such animal at any time before the sale thereof, it shall be the duty of the Pound-keeper to deliver the same on receiving the amount in full of the penalty and necessary expenses incurred for each and every animal. *Impounded animals may be redeemed.*

Sec. 6. It shall be the duty of the Pound-keepers, on making delivery of animal so impounded, before sale, or on payment of surplus money after sale, to obtain from the person or persons claiming the same, his, her, or their name or names, and residence and to enter the same in a book, together with the date when such animal was left, and the date when the same was sold or redeemed, as the case may be. *Duty of pound keeper on delivering the same*

Sec. 7. If no person shall appear to claim such animal or animals so impounded, within five days after the same may have been impounded, or if the the person claiming such animal shall refuse or neglect to pay the penalty and necessary expenses incurred thereon, it shall be the duty of the Pound-keeper to give at least three days' notice of the sale thereof. *Notice of sale.*

Sec. 8. Such notice shall contain a general description of the animal or animals impounded, and shall be posted up in some conspicuous place at the Public Pound where the same shall have been impounded, and also at the several public Markets in the said City. *Form of notice.*

Animals may be sold.

Sec. 9. If, at the expiration of the time specified in the said notice, no person shall appear to claim the animal or animals therein specified and referred to, or if any person shall appear to claim the same, but shall refuse or neglect to pay the penalty and necessary expenses accrued on such animal or animals, the same shall be offered to public competition and sold to the highest bidder by the Pound-keeper at the Pound were the said animal or animals are kept.

Animals may be sold if not paid for.

Sec. 10. If, after the sale of any animal as aforesaid, the purchaser does not immediately pay the price thereof, the Pound-keeper may forthwith cause the animal to be resold, and so continue to do until the price is paid, and shall only give up possession after such payment.

Proceeds of sale, how applied.

Sec. 11. In case of the sale of any impounded animal or animals, the said Pound-keeper shall retain out of the proceeds of such sale sufficient to pay the amount of the penalty, and all necessary expenses incurred by him on account of the said animal or animals.

Owners of animal may redeem the same by paying fees.

Sec. 12. If, after such sale, and whilst the proceeds thereof remain in the hands of the Pound-keeper, the former owner of any animal or animals so impounded and sold, shall appear and claim the proceeds of such sale, it shall be the duty of the Pound-keeper to deduct from the proceeds of such sale the penalty and expenses, as provided in the last preceding section; to ascertain the name and residence of such owner, and to pay over the balance of the proceeds of such sale, if any, to the person so claiming to be the owner, upon satisfactory proof of ownership being given to such Pound-keeper.

Sec. 13. It shall be the duty of each and every Pound-keeper, at the end of each month, to make out and present to the City Clerk a full and detailed report, showing the number of animals received into and discharged from the Public Pound during the year; the particular date when each animal was so received and when each was discharged, and whether the same was redeemed or sold, and if redeemed how much was received by him on account of such animal, and the name of the person from whom it was received, and if sold, how much was paid therefore, the name of the purchaser and the amount of the Pound-keepers expenses thereon, and the balance, if any, remaining over and above such expenses, and to whom paid, and the balance of such moneys remaining in his hands, which balance, if any, shall, prior to making such report, be paid over to the City Treasurer. Monthly returns to be made by pound keepers.

Sec. 14. Any person who shall break open, or in any manner, directly or indirectly, aid or assist in breaking open any Public Pound, or shall take or let any animals out of any Public Pound, without the consent of the Pound-keeper, shall be liable to a fine not exceeding twenty dollars and costs of prosecution and to an imprisonment not exceeding two months, for each offence. Penalty.

Sec. 15. Each and every person who shall hinder, delay or obstruct any person or persons engaged in driving or carrying to any Public Pound any animal or animals liable to be impounded under the provisions of this By-law shall, for each offence, be Ibid.

liable to a fine not exceeding twenty dollars and costs of prosecution and to an imprisonment not exceeding two months.

No. 44.

By-law to prohibit the keeping of Pigs within certain Sections of the City of Montreal.

[*Passed 15th March* 1870.]

Keeping of pigs prohibited within certain limits.

Sec. 1. No person shall rear, keep or feed any pig or swine in the said City of Montreal, save and except within the following boundaries, viz:

FIRSTLY. *"Starting from the City limits, at their instersection with the North-west side of St. Catherine street, thence along the said north-west side of St. Catherine Street to the north east corner of Panet Street; thence along the North easterly side of Panet Street to the City Limits."*

SECONDLY. *"Commencing at the west Corner of McCord and Wellington streets, along the west side of McCord Street to St. Bonaventure Street and thence along the south east side of St. Bonaventure Street to the City limits."*

Penalty.

Sec. 2. Any person offending against the provisions of this By-law shall be liable to a fine not exceeding twenty dollars and costs of prosecution and to an imprisonment not exceeding two months, for each offence.

No. 45.

By-law concerning Sewers.

Passed 15th March 1870

Sec. 1. The said Council may order the construction or repair of any common Sewer or Drain which shall be considered necessary by the Road Committee, in any street or highway. *Council may order sewers to be made.*

Sec. 2. Whenever it shall be determined by the said Council to lay down a Common Sewer, or whenever any street or highway within the said City shall be about to be newly paved or repaired, in which street or highway a Common Sewer shall have been already made and laid, public notice shall be given to the inhabitants and proprietors on such street or highway, specifying the time within which they may avail themselves of making their private drains from their houses or yards into such Common Sewer. *Public notice to be given.*

Sec. 3. The cost of making and constructing any Common Sewer or Drain which shall hereafter be ordered to be made or constructed in any street or highway, or section of a street or highway in the said City, shall be borne and paid by the owners of real estate situated on each side of such street or highway, or section of street or highwey, by means of a special assessment to be made and levied upon the said owners of real estate, according and in proportion to the frontage of their properties respectively; the said assessment to be due and payable immediately after the completion of such Common Sewer or Drain in front of the said properties res- *Cost of sewers, by whom borne.*

Proviso.

pectively: Provided that in no case shall such owners be assessed, whatever the dimensions of such Common Sewer may be, at a higher rate than for their proportion of the cost of a Common Sewer of three feet diameter: Provided also that the said Council may order or permit the construction of tile drains whenever required.

Repairs to sewers to be borne by Council.

Sec. 4. All public Sewers and Drains in this City shall be repaired and kept in order at the expense of the said Council, and all private Drains in connection therewith shall be constructed and kept in order by the proprietors respectively benefited by such private Drains, but under the supervision of the City Surveyor.

Private sewers.

Sec. 5. The Road Committee of the said Council shall have power, in all cases where there is any Common Sewer in any street or highway, to cause every owner of land adjoining such street or highway, or his agent, to make a sufficient drain from his or her house, yard or lot, whenever in their opinion the same shall be necessary, and shall thereupon give such owner or agent notice in writing, through the City Surveyor, specifying the time within which such drain shall be completed; and in case the said owner or agent shall neglect to complete the same within the time specified, the said Committee shall cause the same to be done at the cost and charge of the said owner or agent, the amount of which may be recovered by an action to be brought before the Recorder's Court.

City Surveyor to make plan of sewers.

Sec. 6. It shall be the duty of the City Surveyor, whenever any Common Sewer is ordered to be built or repaired, to ascertain its depth, breadth, mode of construction and general direction, and take the plan thereof, and insert the same with all those particulars, in a book to be kept for that purpose, and forthwith ascertain and insert on said plan all entries made into such Sewer.

Sec. 7. The said City Surveyor shall keep an accurate account of the expense of constructing each Common Sewer, and shall report the same to the Road Committee, together with a list of the persons and estates having a frontage on the street, or highway, or section of a Street, or highway, wherein such Sewer is laid or constructed, accompanied by a schedule shewing the proportion in which such persons and estates are respectively assessed in relation to the cost of the said Sewer. *To keep an account of the same.*

Sec. 8. The said City Surveyor shall enter, in books to be kept for that purpose, all assessments made for defraying the expense of constructing Common Sewers; and after the completion of any such Sewer, he shall forthwith make out bills for the same, and deliver them to the City Treasurer for collection; and the said Treasurer shall forthwith demand payment in writing, of the said bills; and in case any such bills or dues shall remain unpaid at the expiration of twenty days, after demand for payment as aforesaid, the said Treasurer shall cause the same to be collected by a resort to the proper legal process. *Assessments to be entered in a book.*

Sec. 9 No person shall enter his or her private Drain into any Common Sewer without a permit in writing from the City Surveyor; and all persons to whom such permit shall be granted shall pay the *No person to have access to common sewer without permit.*

refor a sum of Three Dollars, if the public drain be constructed of brick, and One Dollar Fifty Cents if the public drain be a wooden one; the amount in each case to include the cost of making the connection, irrespective of the excavation, which shall be done by the proprietors who shall apply for such permit: Provided that if such private drain is constructed within the time specified in the third section of this By-law, so as to allow its connection with the Common Sewer to be made during the construction of the said Common Sewer, and whilst the street is being opened therefor, there will be charged only Two Dollars for such permit, if the connection is to be made in brick, and One Dollar if it be a wooden one.

Private drain how constructed.

SEC. 10. All private Drains shall be laid in such direction, of such size, and with such descent, and (where required) with such strainers as the City Surveyor, under the direction of the Road Committee, shall require; and such Drains shall not, under any pretext, be closed until examined and approved by the City Surveyor.

Connection with common sewer.

SEC. 11. The manner of piercing or opening into any of the Common Sewers or Drains, and the form, size and material of which connections therewith shall be composed, shall be prescribed by the City Surveyor, under the direction of the Road Committee, such connections in no case to be less than three feet in length.

Permission to construct drains, subject to certain conditions.

SEC. 12. The City Surveyor, on application for that purpose, is hereby authorized and empowered to grant permission to persons to construct, at their own expense, Drains to connect with any Common

Sewer built in any of the public streets or highways of the said City; such permission to be conditioned that the persons applying therefor shall comply with the rules, regulations and ordinances of the City in relation to excavating the streets, be responsible for damages or injuries caused to persons, animals or property, by reason of any neglect or carelessness connected with the work permitted, and pay the amount hereinbefore stipulated for such permission.

SEC. 13. All openings into any Common Sewer or Drain, for the purpose of making connections therewith from any private Drain leading to any dwelling house, cellar, yard, or other premises, shall hereafter be made by persons to be licensed by the Road Committee, in writing, to perform such work, and by those persons only; and the said persons, before being so licensed, shall enter into a bond to the Mayor and City Council, in a sufficient penal sum, with surety, conditional that they will carefully make the openings into any Sewers or Drains in the manner and time prescribed by the City Surveyor, without injuring them; that they will leave no obstructions of any description whatever in them, and properly close up the Sewer or Drain around the connection made by them; that they will faithfully comply with the Rules, Regulations, and Ordinances relating to opening and excavating the streets, and be responsible for any damages or injuries that may occur to persons, animals or property, by reason of any neglect or carelessness on their part, connected with said work; provided that the said Committee may at any time revoke such license.

Connections with common sewers to be made by licensed persons.

Sewers to be kept clear.

Sec. 14. No owner or occupant of any dwelling-house, store or other building, or of any manufactory, brewery, distillery, slaughter house or the like, having permission to connect with any public Sewer or Drain as aforesaid, shall permit any substance to flow into any such Sewer or Drain which shall form a deposit having a tendency to fill said Sewer or Drain.

Injuries to sewers punishable.

Sec. 15. No person shall injure, break or remove any portion of any receiving basin, covering-flag, man-hole, vent, shaft, grating, or any part of any Sewer or Drain, or obstruct the mouth of any Sewer or Drain, or obstruct the flow of water in any Sewer or Drain in the said City, under the following penalty.

Penalty.

Sec. 16. Any person offending against any of the provisions of this By-law shall be liable to a fine not exceeding twenty dollars and costs of prosecution and to an imprisonment not exceeding two months, for each offence.

No. 46.

By-law concerning Scavengers.

(Passed 15th March 1870.)

Scavengers to be licensed.

Sec. 1. It shall be the duty of the Board of Health or the Road Committee to let out, by contract, for a term not exceeding five years, to responsible parties, the scavengering of the different Wards of the City.

License for each cart required &c.

Sec. 2. The contractor shall take out a license for each and every cart he may use. Each cart shall have painted, in a conspicuous place on each side thereof, the number of the cart, the figures to be painted black, on a white ground, and to be at least four inches in size; the carts to be tight box carts of a pattern to be approved by the Chief of Police or other Officer appointed by the Board of Health for this purpose.

SEC. 3. The contractor shall remove and take away from each house, within the District assigned to him, all house offal, as hereinafter designated, once a week; the service to be performed between the hours of ten p. m. and eight a. m. *(House offal to be removed &c.)*

SEC. 4. The contractor shall call at each house in his District for the purposes of the present By-Law, and no contractor shall refuse or neglect to remove such house offal as hereinafter designated, nor shall any contractor or his employee behave in an insolent manner or use improper or abusive language in the performance of his duty. *(Contractors to call at each house.)*

SEC. 5. Every householder or tenant must provide a water-tight box, tub, or other vessel, of sufficient size to contain all the house offal that may accumulate, from day to day, on his or her premises, which shall be placed on the sidewalk in front of each house or tenement, or in such convenient spot as may be designated by the Chief of Police or other Officer appointed by the Board of Health for this purpose. Where there are lanes or alleys in rear of houses, the said house offal may be placed therein; and it shall be the duty of the owner or occupant of all houses and tenements to put all their house offal into said boxes, tubs or barrels aforesaid. And each householder, tenant or other person shall put out said house offal in the place so designated, at *(Householders to provide a box for house offal &c.)*

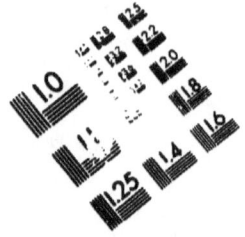 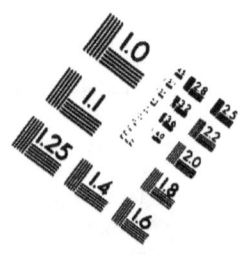

**IMAGE EVALUATION
TEST TARGET (MT-3)**

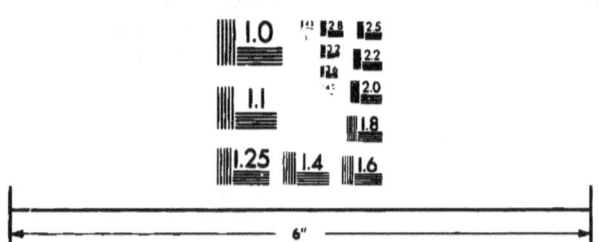

Photographic
Sciences
Corporation

23 WEST MAIN STREET
WEBSTER, N.Y. 14580
(716) 872-4503

the time to be appointed by the Board of Health, for the Scavenger to remove the same.

House offal not to be thrown in street, &c.

SEC. 6. No person shall throw, cast, or lay, or cause to be thrown, cast, or laid, any house offal, filth, manure or rubbish of any kind whatsoever, in any street, lane or alley, private or public, or any public square, place or vacant lot; except the same be placed there for the purposes of and in the manner provided for in this By-Law.

Who is responsible for dirt thrown in streets.

SEC. 7. If any of the substances mentioned in the preceding section shall be thrown or carried from any house, warehouse, shop, cellar, yard or other place, or left in any of the places specified in the preceding section, the occupant, or if there is no occupant, then the owner thereof, shall be held liable for such violation of this by-law, and in the case of terraces, or rows of houses where there is a lane in rear thereof, the occupant of each house shall be responsible for the cleanliness of the portion which is in rear of the house occupied by such occupant. And all such substances shall be removed from the place where they have been so thrown or left, as aforesaid by such occupant as aforesaid, within twenty-four hours after notice in writing to that effect given by the Chief of Police or other officer appointed for this purpose by the Board of Health; or such removal shall be made under the direction of the authority above named and the expense thereof borne by such occupant or owner as aforesaid.

Carts used for carrying "swill."

SEC. 8. Carts, waggons, or other vehicles in or upon which there shall be any hogshead, barrel, cask, box, or other vessel used for removing or carrying "swill" or other offensive matter, shall not be allowed to stand in any street, lane, or alley, longer than is required to receive and take in such "swill" or other matter as aforesaid, under any pretence whatsoever. All such carts shall be water tight, and constructed so that their contents shall not escape into or upon the street; and all such "swill" shall be removed between the hours of eight p. m. and eight a. m.

Sec. 9. The Scavengers shall remove all dead animals or offensive matter, within their respective districts, found lying in the street, or in any other place. *Dead animals.*

Sec. 10. The Scavengers shall deposit the House offal, and dead animals in the manner and in such place or places as may be designated by the Chief of Police or other officer appointed by the Board of Health for this purpose. *House offal where to be deposited.*

Sec. 11. Hotels, restaurants, and public institutions shall pay extra for carrying away any quantity in excess of one barrel; but they shall have the right to contract with any licensed Scavenger for this service. *Hotels, &c., to pay extra charge.*

Sec. 12. House Offal shall include any dead animal, dirt, sawdust, manure, soot, ashes, cinders, shavings, hair, shreds, oysters clam, or lobster shells, and all garbage, whether consisting of animal or vegetable matter, or other offensive substances: Horses, cows and pigs shall be removed at the cost of the owners thereof, where such owners are known. The Scavengers shall have the right to enter all premises and yards during the hour appointed by *House offal definition of.*

the Board of Health, for the purpose of performing the duties assigned to them by the said Board.

Manure how kept. Sec. 13. Manure shall be kept in tight boxes in the yard of the premises where such manure is made. Occupants of Villa Lots in the said City having a superficial area of at least ten thousand feet and part of which is under cultivation, may keep manure for the exclusive use of such lots, provided the same does not inconvenience the neighbours, and subject to such directions and orders as the Health Officer may give in the matter.

Penalty. Sec. 14. Any person offending against any of the provisions of this By-Law shall be liable to a fine not exceeding twenty dollars and costs of prosecution, and in default of immediate payment of the said fine and costs, the defendant may be imprisoned in the common goal for a period not exceeding two months, the said imprisonment to cease upon payment of the said fine and costs.

Expenses how recovered. Sec. 15. The expenses to be incurred under this By-Law, which are chargeable to the owner, occupant, or other person in charge of the premises shall be recovered with costs in the Recorder's Court.

No. 47.

By-law concerning Sidewalks.

[Passed 15th March 1870.]

Dimensions of sidewalks, how regulated. Sec. 1. The City Surveyor is hereby authorized, under the direction of the Road Committee, so to regulate the width and height of the sidewalks of any streets, as shall, in his judgment, be most conducive to the convenience and interest of the City.

Sec. 2. Any person who shall encumber or obstruct any sidewalk, or any street, square, lane, or highway, in the said City, with any article or material whatsoever, without having previously obtained a written permission from the City Surveyor shall forfeit and pay a fine not exceeding Twenty dollars and costs of prosecution, for each offence. *Penalty for encumbering sidewalks.*

Sec. 3. All steps, door-steps, porches, railings, platforms, or other erections projecting into or obstructing any sidewalk, street, square, lane, or highway, within the said City, shall be removed, by and at the expense of the proprietor of the real property on or connected with which such projections or obstructions shall be found, within forty-eight hours after the said proprietor shall have been notified by the City Surveyor to remove the same, under a Penalty not exceeding Twenty Dollars and costs of prosecution for each offence : Provided that conductors from water spouts and windows-guards, not projecting from the face of the wall more than six inches, shall not be taken and considered as projections or obstructions within the meaning of this section. *Projections into streets to be removed by order of City Surveyor.*

Exceptions.

Sec. 4. Whenever any article or material whatsoever, encumbering or obstructing any sidewalk, street, square, lane, or highway, in the said City, shall have been ordered or directed by the City Surveyor to be removed, persuant to the preceding sections of this By-law, and the same shall not be removed within the time limited by such order or *Encumbrances not removed when ordered to be, removed by Surveyor.*

direction, it shall be lawful for the City Surveyor or his deputy, to order the same to be carried or transported at the cost and charge of the parties owning such article or materials, to such place as may be specially allotted by the Council for the reception of all such articles or materials.

Goods for sale or show. Sec 5. No person shall place upon or suffer to be placed upon any sidewalk or street in this City for sale or show, any goods, wares or merchandise whatsoever.

Goods delivered or received. Sec. 6. No person receiving or delivering goods, wares or merchandise, in the said City, shall place or keep upon, or suffer to be placed or kept upon any sidewalk in the said City, any goods, wares or merchandises which he or they may be receiving or delivering, without leaving a passage-way clear upon such sidewalk where such goods may be, sufficient for the use of foot passengers; and no person or persons receiving or delivering such goods shall suffer the same to be or remain on such sidewalk for a longer period than four hours; and any person or persons violating any of the provisions of this or the foregoing section shall be liable to a fine not exceeding twenty dollars and costs of prosecution, for each offence.

Sufficient passage to be kept clear.

Four hours allowed.

Penalty.

Hand barrows not to be used on footpaths. Sec.7. No person shall lead, drive, or ride any horse or other animal, or wheel or drag any hand barrow or hand cart, or push or drag any sleigh or sled, or saw any wood, or in any otherwise needlessly impede any foot-path or sidewalk in the said City, under a Penalty not exceeding Five Dollars and costs of prosecution for each offence.

Sec. 8. Any owner or occupant of any store, house, building, or lot, in the said City, who shall permit or suffer any cart, truck, or any kind of summer or winter vehicle whatsoever, for the purpose of loading or unloading the same with any boxes, crates, casks or packages whatsoever, weighing less than one hundred weight each, to be driven or placed, or backed over or upon the foot-path or sidewalk opposite such store, house, building, or lot, or who shall suffer or permit any cart, truck, or any kind of summer or winter vehicle, for the purpose of loading and unloading the same with any boxes, crates, casks, or packages whatsoever, weighing more than one hundred weight each, to be driven, or placed, or backed over or upon the foot-path or sidewalk opposite such store, house, building, or lot as aforesaid, and remain so for a longer space of time than five minutes at any one time, shall incur and pay a Fine or Penalty not exceeding Five Dollars, and costs of prosecution and an Imprisonment not exceeding forty-eight hours for each offence.

Trucks may be backed over foot-paths in certain cases.

Sec. 9. Whenever any portion of a sidewalk shall have been broken or otherwise injured in consequence of any new building erected or in course of erection on any of the streets or squares in the said City, the City Surveyor shall cause a written or printed notice to be served upon the owner of the said building, calling upon him to repair the damage thus occasioned, by causing the sidewalk in front or adjoining such building, to be put in as good condition as it stood previous to the erection of the said building: Provided the said notice shall require such repairs to be made in forty-eight hours after

Injuries to sidewalks by builders to be repaired.

the service thereof. If such owner shall neglect or refuse to repair the sidewalk as aforesaid, after the said notice, he shall be subject to a Fine not exceeding Twenty Dollars and costs of prosecution, besides being liable for all damages which the City may incur by reason thereof. The City Surveyor shall in all cases, where any proprietor shall refuse or neglect to repair the sidewalks in pursuance of notice as aforesaid, cause the same to be repaired within a reasonable time after the expiration of notice, at the expense of such proprietor against whom the same may be recovered by summary proceeding in the Recorder's Court.

Sidewalks to be kept clean.

SEC. 10. It shall be the duty of the occupant, or in case there is no occupant, of the owner or any person having the care of any building, or lot of land on any street or square in the said City, to keep the sidewalk in front of, or adjoining, such building or lot of land, in a proper state of cleanliness, from the first day of May, to the first day of December, every year, under a Penalty not exceeding Twenty Dollars and costs of prosecution for each offence.

Security against excavations for cellars.

SEC. 11. Any person who shall make or keep open, or cause to be made or kept open, any excavation for cellars or other purposes, on the line of any street or so near thereto as to endanger the safety of foot passengers, shall cause such excavation to be well and properly secured by a substantial railing or covering to the satisfaction of the City Surveyor, during the prosecution of the work.

Cellar doors.

SEC. 12. All proprietors or occupiers, or persons having charge of any house or building in the said City, having cellar doors made on the foot-path or sidewalk opposite their premises, shall constantly keep the said doors in good repair and shut after dark; they shall not leave the said cellar doors open or suffer the same to be left open in the day time for any greater length of time than may be reasonably sufficient for getting into or out of the same such goods, or effects as may be intended to be introduced into or taken out of such cellar; and during the time the said cellar door shall remain open in the day time for the purpose aforesaid, it shall be the duty of the proprietors or occupiers of said premises, to put on each side of the opening of such cellar door a sufficient guard, to be at least three feet high, so as to protect passengers from injury.

Sec. 13. Every entrance or flight of steps, descending immediately from any street, or public way into any cellar or basement story of any building where such entrance or flight of steps shall not be safely and securely covered, shall be enclosed with a railing on each side, permantly put up, at least three feet high from the top of the sidewalk, or pavement together with either a gate to open inwardly, or two iron chains across the front of the entrance way one near the top and the other half way from the ground to the top of the railing; and such gate or chains shall, unless there be a burning light over the steps to prevent accidents, be closed during the night. And any person, who shall be guilty of a violation of any of the provisions of this or the next preceding section, shall be liable to a Penalty not exceeding Twenty Dollars and costs of prosecution which penalty may be recovered of the owner, oc- *Steps descending from street to be enclosed and lighted.*

cupant or other person having charge of such building.

No trees to be planted without permission.

Sec. 14. No person shall plant any tree on any sidewalk or street of the said City, without leave first obtained from the City Surveyor, who shall have power to remove the same, if deemed necessary in the interest of the public.

Snow not to be allowed to accumulate over six inches on sidepaths.

Sec. 15. Whenever, during the winter season, snow or ice shall accumulate on any of the sidewalks in the said City, or any portion of them, it shall be the duty of the person owning, occupying, or having charge of the house, building, or lot of ground, before which such accumulation as aforesaid shall be to cut the said snow or ice down to a depth of six inches above the surface of the said sidewalks, so that the same shall be uniform with that of the adjoining property, unless otherwise ordered, or permitted by the City Surveyor; under a Penalty not exceeding Twenty Dollars, and costs of prosecution for each offence: Provided however that the snow or ice to be removed from such sidewalks may be thrown into the roadway in front of the said house, building or lot of ground; but in doing so, the person owning, occupying, or having charge of such house, building, or lot of ground, shall cause such snow or ice to be broken into small pieces and spread uniformly over the surface of such roadway.

Duty of Surveyor in cases of neglect.

Sec. 16. Should the person owning, occupying, or having charge of any house, building, or lot of land, in the said City neglect or refuse to comply with the provisions of the next preceding section, it shall be the duty of the said Surveyor to cause the work therein ordered, to be done, at the expense of the party guilty of such neglect or refusal, from whom the said Corporation shall recover the amount of the said expense by summary process in the Recorder's Court.

Sec. 17. Whenever the snow shall become so congealed, or ice formed, on any of the sidewalks, or portions thereof, in the said City, as to prove dangerous to passengers, it shall be the duty of the person owning, occupying, or having charge of the house, building, or lot of ground, before which the sidewalks shall be in such state as aforesaid, to cause ashes to be strewed thereon, or the ice or congealed snow to be made rough, by cutting the same, under a Penalty not exceeding Twenty Dollars, and costs of prosecution, for each offence. *Ice on same to be made rough.*

Sec. 18. It shall be the duty of every proprietor or propriters, or company of persons having any cellar shoot, or other aperture, in the streets or sidewalks in the said City, to cause the iron plate or plates, over such shoot or aperture, to be roughed or studded on the exposed surface thereof, or otherwise made so as to prevent danger to passengers therefrom, under a Penalty not exceeding Twenty Dollars, and costs of prosecution for each offence. *Plates over shoots, &c., in streets to be roughed.*

Sec. 19. No person shall place on the mouth of any cellar shoot, or other aperture whatsoever, in any of the squares, streets, lanes, or sidewalks, in the said City, any iron plate or plates not made rough or studded on the outer surface, or otherwise made so as to prevent danger to passengers, under a Penalty not exceeding Twenty Dollars, and costs of prosecution for each offence. *No iron plates to be placed over cellar door unless made rough.*

Snow or ice on roofs to be removed.

Sec. 20. No person occupying or having under his charge any house, part of any house, store-house or part of any store-house, building, or part of any building in this City, shall allow snow to be accumulated, or ice to be formed on the roof of such houses or buildings, or any part thereof, in such a manner as to subject the passers-by to any danger, under a Penalty not exceeding Twenty Dollars, and costs of prosecution and an Imprisonment not exceeding thirty days, for each offence.

Snow on roofs.

Sec. 21. The snow or ice accumulated or formed on the said roofs as aforesaid, shall be removed or thrown down by the party or parties having charge of such houses and buildings, before the hour of nine o'clock in the forenoon; and proper means shall be taken by such party, or parties, in each case, to warn passers-by in the streets of the fact, under a penalty not exceeding twenty dollars, and costs of prosecution and an Imprisonment not exceeding thirty Days, for each offence.

No. 48.

By-law concerning Streets.

[Passed 15th March, 1870.]

Duty of City Surveyor in regard to streets.

Sec. 1. It shall be the duty of the City Surveyor, under the direction and control of the Road Committee, to superintend the general state of the streets, to attend to the laying out, widening, elevation and repairs of the same, and to make all contracts for the supply of labour and materials therefor; and to give notice to the said Committee of any obstruction or encroachment thereon.

Sec. 2. The Council of the said City of Montreal may, and they are hereby authorized, whenever, in their opinion, the safety or convenience of the inhabitants of the City shall require it, to discontinue any street, lane, or alley of the said City, or to make any alteration in the same, in part or in whole. *Power to discontinue streets.*

Sec. 3. It shall be lawful for the persons employed to pave or repave any street in this city, or to construct drains, or other works of a similar nature therein, to place proper obstructions across such street or cartway, for the purpose of preserving the works then newly made, or to be made, until the same shall be fit for use; leaving at all times a sufficient passage for foot passengers. *Streets may be closed to allow public works being made therein*

Sec. 4. When any drain shall be opened or laid, or any aperture shall be made in any street or public square in the said City, the person, or persons, or either of them by whom the said drain shall be opened or laid, or such aperture made, shall cause a rail or other sufficient fence to be placed and fixed so as to enclose such drain, or other aperture and the dirt and gravel or other material thrown into the street; and such fence shall remain during the whole time such drain or aperture shall be open; and a lighted lantern, or some other proper and sufficient light shall be fixed to such part of such fence, or in some other proper manner, over or near such open drain or aperture, and the dirt, gravel or other material taken from the *When any excavation in the streets shall be made &c.*

same, and so kept from the beginning of the twilight of the evening, through the whole of the night, during all the time such drain or aperture shall be open, or in a state of repair, under the penalty of a fine not exceeding twenty dollars and costs of prosecution and an Imprisonment not exceeding two months, for each offence.

Person intending to build to give notice. Sec. 5. Every person intending to erect, or to repair, any building upon land abutting on any of the streets of this City, shall, before proceeding to build or erect the same, or to lay the foundation thereof, or to make the said repairs, give notice in writing to the City Surveyor of such his intention, with the number of the street or precise location, and the name of the owner of the land, eight days at least before doing any act for carrying out such his intention into execution, in order that any encroachment or any other injury or inconvenience to the said public streets, which might otherwise happen, may be thereby prevented; and in default thereof such person shall incur a Penalty not exceeding twenty Dollars, and costs of prosecution.

Allotment to be made by Surveyor for building materials. Sec. 6. Whenever any person or persons shall intend to alter, repair, or erect any building as aforesaid, such person or persons shall apply to the City Surveyor, who shall set off or allot such part or portion of the street, square, lane, or highway, opposite to such ground or the site of such building, as shall be deemed necessary and sufficient for the purpose, and who shall, at the same time, grant a minute in writing of such allotment, in which minute shall be specified the conditions upon which such allotment shall be made; and for every such minute, the party or parties so applying shall pay to the said Surveyor the sum of One Dollar; Provided nevertheless, that the space to be allotted and set off as aforesaid shall not exceed one-third the breadth of the street, square, lane, or highway opposite such ground or building aforesaid, exclusive of the footpath or sidewalk, which shall at all times be kept clear; and the part or portion set off or allotted, and no other part of the said street, square, lane, or highway shall be used for laying down the materials for any such building, or for the repairing thereof, and for receiving the rubbish arising therefrom. And it shall also be the duty of such persons, in all cases, to place at twilight in the evening, suitable and sufficient lights upon such building materials, and keep them burning through the night, until said materials are removed; and all the rubbish arising therefrom or thereby shall be carried away by the person or persons so building, or repairing, at such convenient time as the said Surveyor may direct; and in case of neglect or refusal so to do, it shall be removed and carried away, at the expense of the person or persons so building or repairing; and all persons offending against any of the provisions of this section shall be liable to a fine not exceeding twenty dollars and costs of prosecution and to an imprisonment not exceeding two months, for each offence. *Proviso*

Sec. 7. In all cases where any person or persons shall place building materials in any of the public streets of the said City, such persons shall be answerable for any and every damage, which may be occasioned to persons, animals or property, by *Parties answerable for damages.*

reason of carelessness in any manner connected with the said materials.

Preparing mortar, &c., in streets prohibited.

Sec. 8. No person shall make or prepare mortar, or cut or dress any stone or timber for building purposes, in any street, or public square or place in this City, under a Penalty not exceeding Twenty Dollars and costs of prosecution, and an Imprisonment not exceeding two months, for each offence.

Placing coal or firewood in streets regulated.

Sec. 9. Neither the purchaser nor seller of any Coal or Firewood shall place or permit any such Coal or Firewood to remain in any street, so as unnecessarily to obstruct the passage in the same; nor shall any such coal or wood in any case be permitted, either by the purchaser or seller, or other person having the charge thereof, to lie or continue in any street more than twenty-four hours, under a Penalty not exceeding twenty dollars, and costs of prosecution, and an Imprisonment not exceeding two months, for each offence.

Doors to archways to open inwards

Sec. 10. All Archways constructed on the border of any of the streets, lanes, or public squares of the City and suburbs, and all porches or other entrances into court-yards, shall be closed with doors that shall open into the interior, and not towards the said square, streets, or lanes, so as to leave the passage of the footwalks free at all times; the same to be observed with respect to all gates of gardens, lots or other spaces of ground; the whole under a Penalty not exceeding twenty dollars and costs of prosecution against each and every person, whether proprietor or tenant, offending against the provisions of this section.

Sec. 11. No person shall hereafter place, hang, or suspend at any lesser height than ten feet from the sidewalk or street, nor at any greater distance than two feet in front of, and from the wall of any house shop, store, building, or place whatsoever, any sign, Show-bill or Show-board, under a penalty not exceeding twenty dollars and costs of prosecution, and an imprisonment not exceeding two months, for each offence. *Signs.*

Sec. 12. If any person shall place, affix or continue, in any street, square, lane, or highway of this City, any Awning Posts, or any cloth or canvas for an awning, so as to cause any public inconvenience, or contrary to the directions of the City Surveyor, or his deputy, or shall neglect or refuse to comply with such directions of the said Surveyor or his deputy, such person shall forfeit and pay, for every such offence, a sum not exceeding twenty dollars and costs of prosecution. *Awnings.*

Sec. 13. Any person who, for any purpose whatsoever, shall intentionally place, or cause to be placed, or shall suspend, or cause to be suspended or exposed from any house, shop, store, building or lot abutting on any of the public streets, squares, lanes, or highways of this City, any goods, wares, or merchandize whatsoever, so that the same shall extend or project from the wall in front of such house, shop, store, building, or lot, more than six inches towards or into any public street, square, lane, or highway aforesaid, shall forfeit and pay a sum not exceeding ten dollars and costs of prosecution, for each offence. *Wares suspended from houses.*

BY-LAWS.

Penalty on raising goods from street by tackle.

Sec. 14. No person, whether agent, owner, or employer, shall hereafter suffer or permit any case, bale, bundle, box, crate, or any goods, wares or merchandize to be raised from any street, square, or public place, on the outside of any building, for the purpose of storing the same in the second or any higher story of any such building, or to be lowered from the same in a similar manner, by means of a rope, pulley, tackle, or windlass, under a Penalty not exceeding ten dollars and costs of prosecution, for each offence: Provided, that the provisions of this section shall not be considered or taken to extend to the raising of any materials or other articles necessary in the repairing, erecting, or taking down of any building, or to the removing of any merchandize or other articles, in case of danger by fire or other such casualty.

Street crossings not to be obstructed.

Sec. 15. No person shall place any animal, cart, truck or carriage of any description whatsoever, or any obstructions of any kind, upon or across any of the flags or stepping stones, placed for the convenience of foot passengers, across any street, square, lane, or highway, in the said City, under a penalty of not less than one nor more than twenty dollars and costs of prosecution, for each and every offence.

Large timber not to be dragged on streets.

Sec. 16. All pieces of Timber, which, by reason of their length, cannot be transported in carts or tumbrels, and are usually conveyed on trucks or other vehicles, such as deals, cedars, and other large timber, shall for the future, throughout every part of the City and suburbs, be transported on two trucks or upon such other vehicle so constructed as that the said timber shall not in any manner touch the public way; the whole, under a Penalty not exceeding Ten Dollars and costs of prosecution, against each offender.

Sec. 17. No person shall make, or cause to be made, any aperture in or under any street, for the purpose of constructing Coal Holes, or receptacles for any other article, or for light and air, or for an entrance, or for any other purpose, without the license of the Road Committee, under a Penalty not exceeding Twenty Dollars and costs of prosecution, for each offence, and no person shall leave such Coal Hole or other aperture open or unfastened after sunset, nor in the day time, unless while actually in use with a person or persons at the same to warn passers-by, under the same penalty. *Apertures under street, coal holes, &c*

Sec. 18. No person shall affix or place, or cause to be affixed or placed, or continue, in any street, any Grating, without the license of the Road Committee, under a Penalty not exceeding twenty dollars and costs of prosecution, for each offence. *Gratings in streets.*

Sec. 19. The Road Committee, upon the application of any person, may authorize the construction of Coal Holes or other apertures, and of Gratings, as hereinbefore mentioned, in such manner, and under the direction of such person, as they may deem suitable, at the expense of the applicant; and they may also authorize the continuance of any Grating already constructed: Provided, that in no case shall any Grating be authorized to extend more than eighteen inches into the street. *Coal holes and gratings may be authorized, &c.*

Earth, &c., not to be removed without permission.

Sec. 20. No person shall, without having first obtained a written permission from the City Surveyor, dig, remove or carry away, or cause the same to be done, any sod, stone, earth, sand or gravel from any street, alley or public ground in this City, under a Penalty not exceeding twenty dollars and costs of prosecution, and an Imprisonment not exceeding two Months, for each offence.

Pavements and sidewalks not to be injured.

Sec. 21. No person shall injure or tear up any Pavement, Side or Cross-walk, Drain or Sewer, or shall dig any hole, ditch or drain in any street, pavement or sidewalk, without due authority, or shall hinder or obstruct the making or repairing any Pavement, Side or Cross-walk, which is or may be making under any resolution or order of the Road Committee, or shall hinder or obstruct any person employed by the said Committee or the City Surveyor, in making or repairing any public improvement or work, under a Penalty not exceeding twenty dollars and costs of prosecution, and an Imprisonment not exceeding two months, for each offence.

Boundary stones.

Sec. 22. No person shall cover up or remove any of the Boundary Stones for designating the avenues and streets of the City, under a Penalty not exceeding Twenty Dollars and costs of prosecution, and an Imprisonment not exceeding two Months, for each offence.

Trees.

Sec. 23. No person shall injure or destroy any ornamental or shade Tree, Shrub, Lamp-post, Fence, Railing in or upon any public ground, street alley, or other public place, or upon any private premises, under a Penalty not exceeding twenty dollars and costs of prosecution and an Imprisonment not exceeding two months, for each offence.

Sec. 24. No person shall slide with a sled, train, traineau, or shall skate on any public square, street, or highway in the said City, under a Penalty not exceeding five Dollars, and costs of prosecution and an Imprisonment not exceeding forty-eight Hours, for each offence. Sliding in streets prohibited.

Sec. 25. No person shall play at Foot-ball, or the game commonly called Shinty, or shall throw stones or snowballs in any street, square, or lane of this City, under a Penalty not exceeding Five Dollars, and costs of proseuction and an Imprisonment not exceeding Forty-eight Hours, for each offence. Certain games in streets prohibited.

Sec. 26. Any person who shall climb upon or nitch any horse or other animal to any public Lamp-post, or hang or place any goods, boxes, wood, or any heavy material upon or against the same, or who shall extinguish, or cause to be extinguished, or light, or cause to be lighted, any of said lamps, unless duly authorized so to do, shall be subject to a Penalty not exceeding Twenty Dollars, and costs of prosecution and an Imprisonment not exceeding Thirty Days, for each offence. Penalty for injuring lamp-posts, &c.

Sec. 27. If any trees in any street wherein public lamps are erected, shall be suffered by the owner or the occupant of the premies to grow in such a manner as to obstruct the reflection of the said lamps, it shall be the duty of the City Surveyor, under the direction of the Light Committee, to notify the owner or occupant of the premises forthwith to trim the same, in the manner to be specified in the Trees to be trimmed.

notice; and if any person shall refuse or neglect to comply with such notice, it shall be the duty of the City Surveyor to cause such trees to be trimmed; and the person so neglecting or refusing shall be subject to a penalty not exceeding Twenty Dollars and costs of prosecution, for each offence.

<small>Posting placards.</small> Sec. 28. No person shall post up or affix in any manner any Bill, Placard, or notice, either written or printed, upon the fences, walls, or upon any part of any building in this City (except in cases of expropriation), without the previous consent of the occupants thereof, or if there be no occupants, without the previous consents of the owner thereof; nor upon any part of any building belonging to the Corporation of the said City, without the previous consent of the Mayor, under a Penalty not exceeding Five Dollars, and costs of prosecution and an Imprisonment not exceeding Forty-eight Hours, for each offence.

<small>Numbering of houses.</small> Sec. 29. All houses within the City limits shall be numbered from East to West and from South to North, the even numbers being assigned to the left and the odd ones to the right hand side of each street: in every case of a vacant space intervening, twenty-five feet shall be allowed for a number.

No. 49.

By-law concerning Vaults and Cisterns.

Passed 15*th. March*, 1870.

<small>Permision to construct vaults by whom given.</small> Sec. 1. The Road Committee, on application for that purpose, is hereby empowered to give permission to construct any Vaults or Cisterns in the streets:

provided, in the opinion of a majority of said Committee, no injury will come to the public thereby.

Sec. 2. No person shall cause any Vault or Cistern to be constructed or made in any of the streets in the said City of Montreal, without the written permission of the Road Committee. *No vaults to be made without permission.*

Sec. 3. Every application for permission to erect such Vault or Cistern shall be in writing signed by the proprietor making the same, and shall state the number of square feet of ground which is required for the same and the intended length and width of the same. *Form of application.*

Sec. 4. After obtaining permission to construct or make such Vault or Cistern, and previous to the commencement thereof, the person so applying shall forthwith pay to the City Treasurer the sum of twenty-five cents per each square foot of ground mentioned as required for such Vault or Cistern. *Amount to be paid by applicant.*

Sec. 5. No person shall erect or build, or cause or permit any Vault or Cistern to be made which shall extend further than the line of the sidewalk or curb stone of any street in the said City. *Dimensions.*

Sec. 6. It shall be the duty of every person for whom any Vault or Cistern may be constructing, to cause or procure the same to be measured by the City Surveyor, and to deliver to the Road Committee a certificate of the said measurement, signed by the said Surveyor before the arching of such Vault or Cistern shall be commenced; for each of which certificates the City Surveyor shall be entitled to receive, on behalf of the Corporation of the said City *Regulations as to construction &c.*

from the party requiring the same, the sum of Four Dollars.

Ibid.

Sec. 7. If it shall appear by such certificate or otherwise that such Vault or Cistern occupies a greater number of square feet than shall have been paid for as aforesaid, the owner of such Vault or Cistern shall, in addition to the penalty hereinafter provided, pay twenty-five cents for each square foot of ground occupied by such Vault or Cistern, over and above the number of square feet paid for as aforesaid.

Ibid.

Sec. 8. It shall be the duty of every person or persons engaged in building Vaults or Cisterns as aforesaid, to inclose the ground taken or appropriated for such Vaults, with a fence or railing, in such a manner as to prevent danger to street passengers; and to continue and uphold the said fence or railing until the work shall be completed or the danger removed.

Ibid.

Sec. 9. All Vaults or Cisterns shall be constructed of brick or stone, in a solid and substantial manner and the outward side of the grating or opening into the street shall be either within twelve inches of the outside of the curb stone of the sidewalk, or within twelve inches of the foundation wall of the front of the house or building to which such Vault shall belong.

Grates.

Sec. 10. All grates to vaults shall be made of wrought iron, the bars whereof shall be three-fourths of an inch wide, and one half of an inch thick, and not more than three quarters of an inch apart; or the said Vaults or Cisterns may be provided with thick glass lights, to the satisfaction of the City Surveyor.

Sec. 11. All Vaults or Cisterns shall be completed and the ground and sidewalk over them closed and refitted to the satisfaction of the City Surveyor, within three weeks after they are commenced. *Time for completion*

Sec. 12. It shall be the duty of every proprietor who shall construct, or cause to be constructed, any Vault or Cistern under the provisions of this by-law, to lay and maintain at his own cost, over such Vault or Cistern, a flag stone footpath or sidewalk. *How covered*

Sec. 13. Every proprietor who shall construct, or cause to be constructed, any Vault or Cistern, as aforesaid, shall be answerable for any and every damage which may be occasioned to persons, animals, or property, by reason of carelessness or defect in any manner connected with the said Vault or Cistern. *Damages.*

Sec. 14. No person shall remove, or cause or suffer to be removed, or insecurely fixed, so that the same can be moved in its bed, any grate or covering to the opening or aperture of any Vault in the said City. *Grate and covering.*

Sec. 15. Any person offending against any of the provisions of this bylaw shall be liable to a fine not exceeding twenty dollars and cost of prosecution and to an imprisonment not exceeding two months, for each offence. *Penalty.*

No. 50.

By-law concerning Vehicles.

(Passed 15th March 1870.)

ARTICLE I   HACKNEY CARRIAGES.
ARTICLE II CARTS, TRUCKS, &c.
ARTICLE III VEHICLES IN GENERAL.

ARTICLE. I.

HACKNEY CARRIAGES.

Hackney carriages defined. Sec. 1. Every omnibus, coach, cab, calèche, or other vehicle, whether on wheels or runners, drawn by one or more horses, which shall be used in the City of Montreal for the conveyance of persons for hire from place to place within the said City, shall be deemed a Hackney Carriage within the meaning of this by-law.

License. Sec. 2. No person shall set up, use or drive in the City of Montreal any Hackney Carriage, for the conveyance of persons for hire from place to place within the said City, without having obtained from the Chief of Police a license for such carriage, and a number to be attached to the said carriage, and without having paid the rates and duties severally imposed in and by the tariff contained in the subjoined schedule.

Chief of Police to issue licenses. Sec. 3. The Chief of Police is hereby authorized to grant licenses and numbers to such persons, as he may deem expedient, and who may be duly entitled to the same, to set up, use or drive Hackney Carriages for the conveyance of persons for hire, from place to place within this City, and to demand and exact, for such licenses and numbers the several rates and duties specified in the said tariff; and a record of all licenses so granted shall be kept by the chief of Police, who shall make, at least once a week, a return of all sums so received, and shall pay over the same to the City Treasurer.

Sec. 4. All licenses granted as aforesaid shall expire on the first day of May next after the date thereof. *Licenses when to expire.*

Sec. 5. The owner or driver of any Hackney Coach or carriage shall not be entitled to recover or receive any pay from any person from whom he shall have demanded any greater price or rates than he may be authorized to receive under the present by-law. *Carters not to recover pay in certain cases*

Sec. 6. In case of disagreement as to distance or price, the same shall be determined by the Chief of Police or any of his Deputies in accordance with the tariff *Cases of disagreement, by whom decided.*

Sec. 7. Every owner, driver or other person, having charge of any Hackney Carriage which has a stand in any street or square, shall at all times when driving or waiting for employment, wear the number of his carriage, in brass or plated figures of not less than one inch in size; and the said number shall be placed in the manner directed by the Chief of Police and in such a way that the same may be distinctly seen and read. *Driver to wear numbers.*

Sec. 8. No person, except a licensed owner or driver of any such coach or carriage in the said City, shall wear the number of any such licensed owner or driver; nor shall any person other than a *Duties of owners of carriages.*

licensed driver or owner solicit passengers for any such coach or carriage; nor shall any such licensed owner or driver wear any other than his own number, or suffer or permit any other person to wear the same.

None but licensed carters to wear numbers.

Sec. 9. The following described places shall be the only stands on which it shall be lawful to place for hire, Hackney Carriages in this City, viz:

Stands for hackney carriages.

1.

That part of McGill Street from the south-east corner of Notre-Dame Street to Common Street, provided that the vehicles thereon be in a single line in the middle of the street, with the horses' heads towards Victoria Square, or westwardly.

2.

That part of Dalhousie Square, from the Wicket Gate leading into the Barracks, north-east termination of St. Paul Street, to the street leading down to the Artillery Barracks, provided the vehicles be placed in a straight line, with the horses' heads towards the square, and that all returning vehicles take the stand nearest the said wicket.

3.

That part of Commissioners' Street, from the south-west line of Jacques-Cartier Square to the St. Ann's Market, provided the vehicles be placed in a single line along the harbour revetment wall, with the horses' heads towards the said Market.

4.

That part of Craig Street from Papineau Square to St. Antoine Street, provided the vehicles be placed in a single line, in the centre of the street, with the horses' heads towards the said Square.

5.

The south-east side of Papineau Square, the vehicles to be ranged in a line with St. Mary Street, the the horses' heads towards the Market-place.

6.

The Place d'Armes, for four vehicles on the north, seven on the west, and seven on the east side, facing the Parish Church.

7.

The centre of Jacques Cartier Square, between St. Paul and Commissioners' Streets, the horses' heads to face the Bonsecours Market; and the north east side of said Jacques Cartier Square from Notre-Dame to St. Paul streets, the vehicles to be ranged in a single line along the south side of the street, the horses' heads turned towards Notre Dame Street.

8.

That part of Bonsecours Street from the north-west corner of Notre Dame Street, towards Craig Street, for eight vehicles only, the horses' heads being turned towards Notre Dame Street.

9.

That part of Gosford Street along the Government Garden, for eight vehicles only.

10.

That part of Chaboillez Square next to the Engine House.

11.

The south-west side of that part of Mountain Street immediately below St. Antoine Street, and extending towards St. Bonaventure Street·

12.

The north-west side of that part of Dorchester street immediately above Mountain Street, and extending towards Guy Street, for eight vehicles only.

13.

The north-west side of the said Dorchester Street lying between St. Alexander Street, and within at least two hundred feet of Beaver Hall Square, for six vehicles only : the horses' heads to face the said Square.

14.

That part of Union Avenue from the north-east corner of Ste. Catherine Street towards Sherbrooke Street for eight vehicles only, the horses' heads being turned towards St. Catherine Street.

Clear spaces to be left for cross streets &c. Sec. 10. In every case where the above described stands are intersected by cross streets, rampways or footpaths, clear corresponding places shall be left for the same, but in no case shall the horses or vehicles stationed at any of the said stands, be allowed to remain or stand within twelve feet of any of the said cross streets or the crossings leading thereto ; and all vehicles frequenting such stands, shall close up from the front of each respectively, according to the order of their arrival.

Sec. 11. Whenever the Corporation of the said City may require to take up or use any of the above described stands for the purpose of repairing the roadway, altering the grades thereof, constructing or repairing drains, laying or repairing water pipes, or for any other purposes within the province and privileges of the said Council, the Carters stationed on such stands shall remove their vehicles to such other convenient place as may be assigned to them, for the time being, by the Chief of Police or his Deputies. *Stands may be taken up for repairs to streets, &c.*

Sec. 12. In every case, when any of the above described stands are occupied by the number of vehicles allotted for them, no driver or person in charge of any vehicle shall take, occupy, or possess himself or themselves, of an additional place thereon. *Number of vehicles on stands, limited.*

Sec. 13. The driver, or person in charge of any vehicle exceeding the number hereinbefore allotted to any stand, shall, whenever so required, leave and drive away his horse and vehicle from such stand. *Drivers of vehicles exceeding number allowed, to leave stands.*

Sec. 14. The prices or rates of fare, to be taken by, or paid to the owner, driver or any person having charge of any Hackney Carriage, shall be as follows : *Tariff of fare for hackney carriages.*

BY-LAWS.

PLACES		Two or Four Wheeled Carriage drawn by one horse.		Coaches, or four wheeled Carriages drawn by two horses.		TIME ALLOWED.
FROM.	TO	For one or two persons.	For three or four persons.	For one or two persons.	For three or four persons.	
		$ cts.	$ cts.	$ cts.	$ cts.	
Any Place.	Any other within the same Division and back.	0 15 0 5	0 25 0 00	0 30 0 00	0 40 0 00	½ an hour.
Any Division.	Any place in another Division and back.	0 25 0 35	0 40 0 50	0 40 0 60	0 50 0 75	¾ of an hour. over ¾ of an hour and under one hour.
Any Place.	(Per Hour) Any other in the City.	0 50 0 20	0 70 0 30	0 75 0 30	1 00 0 40	One hour. For every additional ¼ hour.

Drivers not to over charge.

Sec. 15. No such owner, driver, or other person shall demand or exact a higher rate or charge, or higher rates or charges, than that or those specified in the aforesaid tariff; provided that in every description of vehicle each passenger shall be allowed a reasonable weight of luggage free of charge, and that children under twelve years of age shall only be charged half price

Tariff not to preclude private arrangement.

Sec. 16. The above tariff shall not be taken or held to supersede any specific arrangement which parties hiring such vehicles, as aforesaid, may make with drivers or owners thereof.

No person shall refuse to pay the tariff fare.

Sec. 17 No person or persons who shall or may employ any licensed carter, or cause himself, or themselves, or his, her, or their effects, to be carried conveyed, or driven in any public-licenced vehicle in the said City, shall refuse to pay the just and established fare therefor, or the fare agreed to be paid therefor.

BY-LAWS. 217

Sec. 18. There shall be affixed by the owner or driver of each and every Hackney Carriage, in a conspicuous place in the inside thereof, a card, on which shall be printed the above tariff of rates, with the number of the vehicle and name of owner legibly written thereon. *Tariff to be posted in the carriage.*

Sec. 19. The provisions of the foregoing sections of this By-law shall apply, and be held to apply, to Sleighs and winter vehicles of that description which shall use any of the stands aforesaid. *Provisions extended to sleighs.*

ARTICLE II.
CARTS, TRUCKS, &c.

Sec. 20. Each Cart, Truck, Waggon, Dray, *diable*, or corresponding winter vehicle, and every other vehicle, which shall be used within the City of Montreal for the conveyance from place to place, within the said City, of wood, coal, lumber, slate, stone, brick, lime, sand, gravel, clay, bread, biscuits, milk, beer, porter, ale, whisky, spirituous liquors, goods, wares, furniture, merchandise, building materials, or any other article, or thing whatsoever, whether of a like description or not, shall be licensed, as hereinafter provided, and shall have placed upon the same, the number of the licence in plain legible figures of not less than one inch in size, and so that the same may be distinctly seen ; and if the owner of any such vehicle shall use, or suffer the same to be used, or if any other person shall use any such vehicle, without being licensed as hereinafter provided, or without having the number so placed as aforesaid, or without having paid for such license and number the rates and duties severally imposed in and by the tariff contained in the sub- *License.*

joined schedule, they or either of them shall be liable to the penalty hereinafter provided.

Chief of Police may grant licenses

Sec. 21. The Chief of Police is hereby authorized to grant licenses to such persons as may be deemed entitled to the same, to use and to drive, any such vehicle as aforesaid, within the City of Montreal, and to demand and exact for such licenses and numbers, the several rates and duties specified in the said tariff; and a record of all licenses so granted shall be kept by the Chief of Police, who shall make at least once a week a return of all sums so received, and shall pay over the same to the City Treasurer.

License, when to expire.

Sec. 22. All licenses granted, as aforesaid shall expire on the first day of May next, after the date thereof.

Manner of numbering.

Sec. 23. The Chief of Police shall fix and determine the place or places on the said vehicles where the said numbers shall be attached, and the manner in which the same shall be so attached to the said vehicles; and no owner or driver of any vehicle as aforesaid, shall use, or suffer such vehicle to be used with any other number upon the same than that determined upon and specified by the said Chief of Police.

Stands for carts, trucks, &c.

Sec. 24. The following described places shall henceforth be the only stands in this City on which it shall be lawful to place for hire Carts, Trucks, Waggons, and such like vehicles, and corresponding winter vehicles, namely:

Firstly,—That part of Commissioners' Street along the harbour revetment wall, from Jacques-Cartier Square to Youville Street; provided the vehicles be ranged in a single line, with the horses' heads directed up the driver.

Secondly,—That part of Commissioners' Street, from the Custom House Square to the Canal Basin, the vehicles being ranged in single line, with the horses' heads directed towards McGill Street.

Sec. 25. In every case where the above described stands are intersected by cross streets, rampways or footpaths, clear corresponding spaces shall be left for the same. When stands are intersected by streets.

Sec. 26. The said City shall, for the purposes of this By-law, be divided into three divisions, as follows : City divided into three divisions

The First Division shall comprise the East, Centre and West Wards, (including the South-West side of McGill street and the North-West side of Craig Street,) and shall be subdivided into two sections, Eastern and Western, the line of demarcation between them being the centre of St. Lambert and St. Jean Baptiste Streets.

The Second Division shall comprise the St. Ann, St. Antoine, and St. Lawrence Wards (exclusive of McGill and Craig Streets).

The Third Division shall comprise the St. Louis Ward (exclusive of Craig Street), the St. James and St. Mary's Wards.

Sec. 27. The following shall be the Tariff of rates or charges for all Carts, Trucks, Waggons, or other such vehicles, for public hire, in this City; and it shall not be lawful for the drivers or owners of any such Carts, Trucks, Waggons or other such vehicle for public hire in this City, to demand or exact for the transport or conveyance of any goods, wares, merchandise, or effects whatsoever, from any one place to any other or others, in the said City, higher rates or charges than the same, viz :— Tariff of fares for cartage.

TARIFF OF CARTAGE.

GENERAL RATES.

DESCRIPTION OF GOODS.	CONTENTS OR LOAD.	From any place to any other in the 1st Division, or from any place (exclusive of the Harbour wharves) to any place in the City and vice-versa provided the distance do not exceed ¾ of a mile.	From any of the Harbour wharves to any place in the 2nd or 3rd division within ½ a m. distance from the boundary line of the 1st division and vice-versa, or from any place (exclusive of the wharves) to any other in the City and vice-versa, provided the distance do not exceed 1¼ mile.	For every additional half mile.
		Cts.	Cts.	
Articles not herein enumerated (of a convenient bulk)..................	Not over 1,500 lbs. weight			
Ashes, Pot or Pearl.................	Two barrels..................			
Beef, Pork or Fish...................	Five barrels of 3 tierces...			
Coals or Coke.......................	Half a chaldron or ½ a ton	15	25	
Crockery............................	One crate or 1 hogshead...			
Flour or Fruit......................	Seven barrels...............			
Grain...............................	Not over 1,500 lbs. weight			
Lumber-Sawn, from yard or boat...	500 feet, board measure....			10
Salt or Rice........................	Six bags or 6 barrels.......			
Firewood-dry from boat or yard....	Half a cord 3 feet long.....			
" green or " from rafts..	" " "			
Furniture or Luggage...............	Per load....................			
Lumber-green or hard from rafts...	500 feet, board measure....	20	30	
Molasses, Sugar or Oil..............	One puncheon, hogshead or load............			
Pig Iron, Lead, Copper or Tin......	One ton.....................	25	35	
Bar Iron or Steal....................	"	30	40	

SPECIAL RATES.

	To	FROM	
		Any place in the Western Section of the First Division.	Any place in the Eastern Section of the First Division.
		Cts.	Cts.
And vice-versa for one load,	The stores and wharves below Wellington bridge, south side of Lachine Canal...................	20	25
	The stores and wharves below Wellington bridge north side of Lachine Canal..................	25	30
	The basins above Wellington bridge, north side of Lachine Canal........	25	30
	The basins above Wellington bridge, south side of Lachine Canal, and the Stores, Stations, Factories, &c., at Point St. Charles.............	35	40
	The Stores, Factories, &c., at and above St. Gabriel Locks north of Lachine Canal...................	30	35
	The St. Bonaventure Street Railway Station.........................	20	25
	" from the lower wharves of the Harbour..............	25	30

For any excess over the quantity or weight fixed for a load, additional *pro rata* rates shall be paid.

If delay is caused to the Carter by the employer beyond the time usually required for loading, the Carter shall be paid *extra* for such delay at the rate of five cents for every quarter of an hour.

If a Carter is called, and there be no load ready for him, or if he be unable to load the goods or articles for want of assistance, he shall be paid as if he carried a load the distance thus unnecessarily travelled.

ARTICLE III.

VEHICLES IN GENERAL.

Sec. 28. No Carriage or Vehicle of any description, whether of burden or pleasure, shall be driven through any part of the City of Montreal during any time that the snow or ice shall be upon or cover the streets of the said City, unless there shall be two or more bells attached to the horse or horses, or some part of the harness thereof. *Bells required in certain cases.*

Sec. 29. No person driving any Carriage or Vehicle, or riding any horse, mare, gilding or other beast in or through the said City, shall permit the beast or beasts to run, gallop, trot, pace or go at any rate exceeding six miles to the hour, or in a careless or reckless manner. *Pace at which horses shall go.*

Sec. 30. No owner, driver, or other person having the care of any Truck, Cart, Waggon or other Vehicle, whether used for burden or pleasure, shall stop or place such vehicle at or near the intersection of any street, lane or alley, in such manner as to cross the footing or flag stone, or prevent foot passengers from passing the street, lane or alley in the direction or line of the footway or flagstone on the side of such street, lane or alley. *Carriages shall not stop so as to obstruct foot passengers.*

Sec. 31. No person shall drive any horse faster than a walk, when coming out of any cross street or court-yard into any of the main or leading streets in the said City, or in turning any corner of a street in the same. *Horses to walk in coming out of cross streets, &c.*

Sec. 32. No person shall use any wheel-carriage on the streets of the said City, during the winter, after the City Surveyor shall have given public notice, prohibiting the use of all such wheel-carrages *No wheel carriages to be used after notice from Surveyor.*

within the City, which prohibition shall continue until a notification to the contrary is issued by the said officer.

Drivers to be specially licensed. Sec. 33. All drivers of any public vehicle of any kind whatsoever shall be personally and specially licensed for that purpose in the manner herein before provided, and no person shall drive any public vehicle without being provided with such license and with a corresponding number; and every such driver of a public vehicle shall, whenever required, exhibit the number given to him on taking his license.

Their qualification. Sec. 34. All licensed drivers as aforesaid, shall be properly qualified for the business from age and experience, and each capable of controlling the horse in his charge, and they shall all be provided with good sound horses, and with subtantial vehicles and harness.

Licenses subject to forfeiture. Sec. 35. All licenses, whether to owners or drivers of vehicles as aforesaid, shall be liable to forfeiture, for incompetency or misconduct, or on conviction of drunkeness or any other misdemeanor.

Carters not to carry dead bodies in their vehicles. Sec. 36. No licensed carter shall carry any dead body or allow his cab or other covered vehicle to be used for the purpose of carrying any dead body.

Drivers to exhibit tariff. Sec. 37. Every driver of any public licensed Vehicle for hire in the said City, shall, when required so to do, by any passenger, in such Vehicle, exhibit a copy of the tariff of rates of conveyance hereinbefore mentioned.

Drivers to give number of vehicle. Sec. 38. Every owner, driver, or person having charge of any Vehicle aforesaid, in the said City, shall, upon being requested so to do, give the number of his vehicle, the name of the owner thereof, and his place of abode.

Sec. 39. No person having charge of any Vehicle, on any of the stands aforesaid, shall wantonly snap or flourish his whip, or needlessly leave such Vehicle, or annoy passengers in the street by seeking for employment. *Shall not snap or flourish whip, &c.*

Sec. 40. Every carter, or driver of any public licensed Carriage or Vehicle for hire when unemployed, shall be held to accommodate the first person who shall offer him employment; and no carter or other person aforesaid when unemployed shall loiter about, or remain on any other place than on one of the stands aforesaid. *Carters to accommodate first applicant.*

Sec. 41. No carter shall make use of, for hire within the said City, any Cart or Tumbrel, that shall contain less than two hogsheads, except in cases hereinafter provided and which shall not have been previously measured and stamped by the Chief of Police. *Carts or tumbrels.*

Sec. 42. All Tumbrels used for the carting of lime shall be capable of containing three bariques, and those for sand two bariques, in both cases to be stamped, in the manner designated in the preceding section. *Tumbrels for carting lime.*

Sec. 43. All Tumbrels, or other such Vehicles, used in the said City, for the transport of loose or liquid materials, shall be so constructed as not to drop or lose any of the load in the streets; and no person shall hereafter use or drive in any part of the City, any Tumbrel or other such Vehicle if otherwise constructed than as herein provided. *Tumbrels for loose materials.*

Carts, trucks, &c., to have drivers.

Sec. 44. Every Cart, Truck, or such like Vehicle, shall be provided with a driver. It shall, however, be allowable for one driver to have charge of two such, when the led horse and cart are securely attached to the one preceding it.

Policemen to visit stands.

Sec. 45. It shall be duty of the Chief of Police, and of the officers and men under his command, to visit the public stands and places where Vehicles for hire are permitted to stand; and thereat, as well as elsewhere, at all times, and in all places in the said City, to enforce the rules and regulations respecting such Vehicles, and the drivers thereof, and to maintain order amongst the same, and to report to the Clerk of the Recorder's Court all offenders against any of the provisions of this By-law.

Exchange of numbers prohibited.

Sec. 46. No person shall exchange, or lend out, his number, or numbers for which licenses have been taken out; neither shall any person have a number on his horse, different from the number attached to the Vehicle.

Drivers to remain near vehicles.

Sec. 47. It shall not be lawful for the drivers of Vehicles frequenting the public stands in the said City, or any of them, to stray or absent themselves from the Vehicle or Vehicles under their charge.

Licenses to specify vehicles.

Sec. 48. In each and every of the licenses for Carriages or Vehicles, kept or used for hire within the said City, by others than livery stable keepers to be hereafter issued, the kind of summer or winter Vehicle for which such licenses shall be taken out, shall be distinctly mentioned; and no person shall hereafter, use for hire any kind of Vehicle within the said City, being of a different kind from that for which such person shall have a license as aforesaid, or permit any person in his employ so to do.

Sec. 49. No person shall forge or fraudulently multiply any of the numbers issued under the authority of the Chief of Police, for Vehicles for hire, in the said City; neither shall any person make or cause to be made, a copy or copies of the same, or shall have affixed to his horse or Vehicle, any number or numbers which have not been so issued. *Forgery of numbers, &c.*

Sec. 50. No person shall obliterate, deface, reverse, cover over, or by any contrivance conceal or render illegible, the number or numbers of his Vehicle or Vehicles, or permit the same to be done. *No person shall obliterate numbers*

Sec. 51. Every person, being the owner or owners of any Vehicle or Carriage, for hire in the said City, who shall prefer to have the number or numbers for which a certificate or certificates of registry has or have been procured, painted on any such Vehicle or Vehicles, shall be required to apply for and obtain the leave of the Chief of Police of the said City, so to paint the said number or numbers on any such Vehicle or Vehicles; and shall, moreover, in every such case, after leave has so as aforesaid been obtained, be further required to cause the same to be painted on such Vehicle or Vehicles so as to correspond as to size and colour with the tickets of numbers issued under the authority of the said Chief of Police. *Numbers may be painted on vehicles.*

Sec. 52. Each and every person hereafter applying for a license under this By-law shall, if required, before obtaining the same, produce and file a testimonial or certificate, which shall be satisfactory to *Testimonial of good conduct to be produced if required.*

226 BY-LAWS.

the Chief of Police, of his honesty, sobriety, and upright character, and of his capacity and means to keep a good horse and Vehicle.

Master carters liable for misconduct of drivers.

Sec. 53. Master carters, employers and owners of horses and Vehicles, shall in all cases, be liable for the misconduct or negligence of their servants, drivers, or persons in their employ, or having charge of their horses or Vehicles; and for each offence committed by their said servants, drivers, or other persons in their employ, or having charge of their horses or Vehicles, against any of the provisions of this By-law, the said master carters, employers, and owners of horses and Vehicles shall be liable to the same fine and penalty as are therein and thereby imposed upon the said servants or drivers, or other persons aforesaid, the actual offenders.

Penalty.

Sec. 54. Any person offending against any of the provisions of this By-law shall be liable to a fine not exceeding twenty dollars and costs of prosecution and to an imprisonment not exceeding two months, for each offence.

Tariff of rates and duties to be paid by carters, &c.

Sec. 55. The several rates enumerated and specified in the Tariff contained in the subjoined Schedule shall be the rates which the Chief of Police shall be and is hereby authorized to annually demand and exact for the license for any of the Carriages or Vehicles therein mentioned.

(Schedule.)

TARIFF OF RATES.

To be collected annually by the Chief of Police for licenses issued to carters and others using hackney-carriages or vehicles for the conveyance of passengers, or the transport of goods, wares, merchandise, building materials, produce or other articles, in the City of Montreal.

HACKNEY CARRIAGES.

1. For every Cab, Caleche, or other two wheeled vehicle—*Five dollars*.................. $5.00
2. For every four wheeled Carriage drawn by one horse—*Seven dollars*...... .... 7.00
3. For every coach or four wheeled Carriage drawn by two horses—*Nine dollars*......... 9.00
4. For every Omnibus or Stage coach—*Sixteen dollars*...................................... 16.00

CARTS, TRUCKS, WAGGONS AND OTHER VEHICLES.

The licenses for Carts, Trucks, and other vehicles used for the conveyance of goods, wares, merchandise, etc., shall be divided into three classes, as follows:

The first class shall include all Carts, Waggons, and other vehicles running within the City for hire or reward not otherwise expressly provided for, and shall pay:—

5. For every Cart, Truck, or other two wheeled vehicle—*Two dollars*.............. ...... 2.00
6. For every Waggon or four wheeled vehicle drawn by one horse—*Six dollars*......... $6.00
7. For every Waggon or four wheeled vehicle drawn by two horses, and made to carry a load under 4.000 lbs. weight — *Seven dollars* 7.00

8. For every waggon, float or other four wheeled vehicle drawn by two or more horses, and made to carry heavy articles or materials weighing 4,000 lbs, or upwards. —*Nine Dollars*.. 9.00

9. For every Diablo............... .... 4.00

10. The second class shall include all Carts, Waggons or other vehicles used by Merchants, Traders, Manufacturers, Contractors for the conveyance or delivery of the articles or effects dealt in, manufactured or made use of by them, for each of which there shall be paid, in addition to the rates charged for in the first class.—*Two dollars and fifty cents*.. 2.50

11. The third class shall include all Carts, Waggons, or other vehicles used by Expressmen, Bakers, Brewers, Distillers, Farmers or Gardeners, for each of which there shall be paid, in addition to the rates charged for in the first class—*Five dollars*... 5.00

Parties obtaining licenses, as aforesaid, shall moreover pay the annual assessment on all working horses employed in drawing the above mentioned vehicles or Carriages, at the rate of *two dollars* and *fifty cents* ($2,50) each, and also twenty-five cents for each number granted by the Chief of Police.

The same rates shall apply to all corresponding winter vehicles.

No. 51.

By-law to provide for the Care and Management of the Montreal Water Works, and to establish a Tariff of Water Rates.

[Passed 15th March 1870.]

Sec. 1. The Water Department of this City shall be under the direction of the Water Committee. <small>Water Department, under whose direction.</small>

Sec. 2. The Superintendent of the Water Works shall take such charge of the Aqueducts, reservoirs, and other works and property, as well as of all plans belonging to or connected with the Water Works, as the Water Committee may from time to time direct; and he shall perform all such services in relation thereto, as may be required of him, by the said Committee, or the City Council. <small>Superintendent to have charge of aqueducts, &c.</small>

Sec. 3. The said Superintendent shall, on or before the fifteenth day of March, annually, present to the City Council a report of the general condition of the Water Works and such other matter as he, or the Water Committee, may deem expedient, accompanied by any information or suggestion, which he or they may deem necessary. <small>He shall make an annual report.</small>

Sec. 4. The said Superintendent, or any of his deputies, may enter the premises of any Water Tenant, to examine the water pipes and apparatus, the quanity of water used, and the manner of use. <small>City's agents may enter premises, &c.</small>

Sec. 5. The introduction of the said Water into all buildings to be supplied by the said Water Works, shall be made by and at the expense of the said Council; but the distribution of the Water in <small>Introduction of water and distribution pipes.</small>

all such buildings shall be made by and at the expense of the proprietors thereof; and whenever any such building may be occupied by a tenant and the proprietor thereof shall refuse or neglect to provide for the said distribution, such tenant may, in case the said Council shall exact from him the payment of the rate imposed as aforesaid, withhold from the said proprietor, out of the rents to be paid to him, the sum thus paid by such tenant, unless there be an agreement to the contrary between them.

Tenants to keep pipes in good repair. Sec. 6. All persons taking the water shall keep the distribution pipes within their premises in good repair, and protected from frost, at their own expense; and they shall be held liable for all damage which may result from their failure to do so.

To prevent waste, &c. Sec. 7. Water Tenants shall prevent all unnecessary waste of water, and there shall be no concealment of the purposes for which it is used.

No alteration to be made, except, &c. Sec. 8. No alteration shall be made in any of the pipes or fixtures inserted by the City, except by its agents or officers.

Water not to be supplied to other parties, &c. Sec. 9. No water is allowed to be supplied to parties not entitled to it under this By-law, unless by special permission from the Water Committte.

Hydrants. Sec. 10. No person, unless duly authorized by the said Committee, shall open any hydrant in the said City, or lift or remove the cover of, or draw water from the same.

Turning on or turning off of water. Sec. 11. No person shall turn on or turn off the water in any manner, or interfere with any of the water pipes or valves belonging to the City, without the license of the Water Committe, or of the said Superintendent.

Sec. 12. No person shall pass the Railing enclosing the Reservoirs of the said City, or shall defile, or deposit any filth or offensive matter in the said Reservoirs, or on the bank or ground adjacent thereto, belonging to the said City, or shall allow any dog or other animal, to go or jump into the said Reservoirs, or upon the said bank or ground; or shall pass or remain upon the said bank or ground after ten o'clock in the evening; or shall do, or cause anything to be done tending to defile or corrupt, to disturb or agitate the waters of the said Reservoirs. *No person to interfere with reservoirs, &c.*

Sec. 13. No person shall draw water from the River St. Lawrence for the purpose of selling the same in any part of the City. *No person to sell water from the river.*

Sec. 14. No person shall draw or use water from the Water Works in the said city, for private fountains, or for hand hose for watering purposes, or for building or manufacturing purposes, unless such person shall have previously obtained from the Superintendent of the said works a written permission to that effect and paid the respective rates charged in the subjoined tariff for the supply of water in such cases. *Water for building purposes and not to be used without permission.*

Sec. 15. No metre shall be used for determining the quantity of water supplied by the said works, unless the same shall have been previously submitted to and approved by the said Superintendent. *Metre to be approved of.*

Sec. 16. The several rates enumerated and specified in the Tariff contained in the subjoined schedule, shall be and the same are hereby imposed for water to be supplied from the Water Works of the said City. *Water rates established.*

By whom payable.

Sec. 17. The said rates shall be due and payable to the City Treasurer, in advance, on the fifteenth day of August every year, by the occupant or lessee, or occupants or lessees of all buildings, part of buildings or tenements in the said City, supplied with water from the said works, as well by those who shall consent as by those who shall refuse to receive the water pipe to supply the said water, or to use the same.

Charges for specific supplies.

Sec. 18. All charges for specific supplies, or for fractional parts of the year, shall be payable in advance, and before the water is let on.

Supply may be cut off.

Sec. 19. In all cases of non-payment of the rates imposed by the preceding By-law for thirty days after the same are due, the said Council or any duly authorized officer charged with the management of the said Works, may cut off the supply of Water from any building upon which the said rates shall be due, which shall not prevent the said rates from running as before; and the Water shall not be let on except upon payment of all arrears due.

Penalty.

Sec. 20. Any person offending against any of the provisions of this By-law shall be liable to a fine not exceeding twenty dollars and costs of prosecution and to an imprisonment not exceeding two months, for each offence.

SCHEDULE.

TARIFF OF WATER RATES.

DWELLING HOUSES.

For every Tenement or Dwelling House occupied by one family only:

Per Annum.

1.—When assessed at an **amount not** exceeding $30 per annum, *Five Dollars*...... $5.00
2.—When assessed at an amount exceeding $30 but not over $40.. .... $5.75
3.—When assessed at an amount exceeding $40 but not over $50...................... $6.50

And so on, continuing according to the same scale, that is to say, adding for every additional sum of $10 or any part thereof, *seventy-five cents*............ $0.75

For every additional family lodging in or occupying any part of such Tenement or Dwelling House, an additional rate shall be exacted, equal to one-third of the rate imposed for a single family.

STORES, SHOPS, OFFICES. ETC.

Per Annum.

For each House, part of a House or Tenement occupied as a Store, Shop, Office, Warehouse, Manufacture, or other place of business, with the exception of Retail Groceries:

1.—When assessed at an amount not exceeding $50 per annum, *Four Dollars*........ $4.00

2.—When assessed at an amount exceeding
$50 but not over $75...................... 5.00
3.—When assessed at an amount exceeding
$75 but not over $100...................... 6.00
And so on, continuing according to the same scale, that is to say, adding for every additional sum of $25 or any part thereof, *One Dollar*....................... 1.00

HOTELS OR TAVERNS.

For every Hotel or Tavern:
1—When assessed at an amount not exceeding $100 per annum, *Twelve Dollars*... 12.00
2.—When assessed at an amount exceeding $100 but not over $150.................... 17.00
3.—When assessed at an amount exceeding $150 but not over $200.................... 22.00
And so on, continuing according to the same scale, that is to say, adding for every additionnal sum of $50 or any part thereof, *Five Dollars*.................. 5.00

STABLES.

In Private Stables—including water for washing Carriages, if there be any:
For each Horse.. 3.00
Carter's Stables:
For each Horse, owned by a Carter or Truckman, or driven in a Cart, Truck, *Diable*, or such like vehicle...................... 1.50
For each Horse owned by a cab man, or driven in a cab, Coach, or such like public vehicle 2.00

In Livery Stables:

For each Horse kept for hire...............	1.50
For every unoccupied one horse Stall in such Stables...............	0.50

In Stables in which horses, the property of persons residing within the limits of the City, are kept, fed and groomed:

For each Horse...............	3.00
For every unoccupied Stall...............	0.50

In Stables for the keeping, feeding, and grooming of horses, belonging to persons residing beyond the City limits:

For each one horse Stall...............	0.50
For each Cow kept in the City...............	1.00

STEAM ENGINES.

For every stationary high pressure Engine, working not over twelve hours per day:

For each horse power...............	7.00
Or for every 100 gallons of water (the supply to be determined by *metre* to be furnished by the occupants)...............	0.03

For every stationary low pressure Engine:

For every 100 gallons of water (the supply to be determined as above, by metre, furnished by the occupants)...............	0.03

For the supply of Locomotive Engines belonging to Railroad Companies; or the Engines used in Breweries, Distilleries, or any other manufactory or for any other purpose whatsoever not specially provided for in the present Tariff:

BY-LAWS.

For every 100 gallons of water (the supply to be determined by metre furnished by the occupants).............................. 0.03

All rates imposed as above for Steam Engines shall be distinct and separate from any other rate for water imposed upon the premises.

Where there is no metre, the supply to be charged for upon an estimate to be made by the Water Commitee of the quantities used each day.

FOUNTAINS.

Fountains shall only be supplied with water at the discretion of the Water Committee, and when so supplied shall be charged as follows:

For every 100 gallons of water $0.03

The quantity used to be determined in all cases by the estimate of the Water Committee or by metre.

WATER CLOSETS.

	Per Annum.
For each Closet, with Tank and Service Box	4.00
For each Closet without Tank, but with Self-closing Valve.....	6.00
For each Closet supplied with water by any means whatsoever, but different from those above specified........	15.00

BATHS.

Public Baths, or Baths for the use of which a charge is made by the occupants—for each tub... 6.00

HOSE.

For the right to attach and use a Hose of not more than three-eighths of an inch orifice, for watering the streets, &c.....	1.00

BUILDING PURPOSE.

For every thousand Bricks used, the water therefor to be charged (Payable in advance)...............................	0.10
For every toise of Masonry, the Water therefor to be charged (Payable in advance)	0.05
For every thousand yards of Plastering "	5.00

When Water is required for purposes not specified in the foregoing Tariff, the rate shall be fixed by the Water Committee.

The Water Committee shall have power to ascertain, by metres, the quantity of Water used in any of the above cases, and charge accordingly.

No. 52.

By-law to repeal the several By-laws therein mentioned.

[Passed 15th March 1870.]

The By-law of the Council of the City of Montreal number one passed on the twenty third day of January one thousand eight hundred and sixty six and intituled " *By-law to amend By-law chapter thirty concerning sidewalks ;*" the By-law of the said Council number eight, passed on the fourth day of February one thousand eight hundred and sixty-seven and intituled " *By-law to impose a duty on billiard* (By-laws repealed.)

tables ;" the By-law of the said Council, chapter eight, passed on the tenth day of May, one thousand eight hundred and sixty five and intituled " *By-law in relation to the manufacture and sale of bread ;* the By-law of the said Council, chapter nine, passed on the tenth day of may, one thousand eight hundred and sixty five and intituled " *By-law concerning the erection of buildings ;* the By-law of the said Council, chapter Twelve, passed on the tenth day of may, one thousand eight hundred and sixty-five and intituled " *By-law to regulate the sale and measurement of coal.*"; the By-law of the said Council, number twenty-two, passed on the seventh day of June one thousand eight hundred and sixty-nine and intituled " *By-law concerning dogs ;* " the By-law of the said Council number five, passed on the eleventh day of September one thousand eight hundred and sixty-six and intituled " *By-law of the Council of the City of Montreal to prevent carters from transporting dead bodies in covered carriages ;*" the By-law of the said Council, number eleven passed on the eighth day of May one thousand eight hundred and sixty-seven and intituled " *By-law concerning the organization of the Fire Department ;*" the By-law of the said Council, chapter sixteen, passed on the tenth day of May, one thousand eight hundred and sixty-five and intituled " *By-law concerning firewood ;*" the By-law of the said Council, chapter seventeen, passed on the tenth day of May, one thousand eight hundred and sixty-five and intituled " *By-law concerning offences against good morals and decency ;*" the By-law of the said Council, chapter seven, passed on the tenth day of May, one thousand eight hundred and sixty-five and intituled " *By-law to establish a Board of Health in the City of Montreal* ;" the By-law of the said Council, number twenty three passed on the seventh day of June one thousand eight hundred and sixty-nine and intituled " *By-law concerning the sale of milk* ; " the By-law of the said Council, ch̄ r twenty-one passed on the tenth day of May, one thousand eight hundred and sixty-five and intituled " *By-law concerning nuisances* ;" The by-law of the said Council, number sixteen, passed on the ninth day of June one thousand eight hundred and sixty-eight and intituled " *By-law concerning Sinks, Privies and Cess-Poolls* ;" article second of the By-law of the said Council, chapter fifteen, passed on the tenth day of May one thousand eight hundred and sixty-five and intituled " *By-law concerning the Fire Department* ;" the By-law of the said Council, chapter twenty-three passed on the tenth day of Ma   ne thousand eight hundred and sixty-five and   .tuled " *By-law to preserve public peace and good order* ;" the By-Law of the said Council, chapter twenty-five passed on the tenth day of may one thousand eight hundred and sixty-five and intituled "*By Law Concerning public pounds*" ; the By-Law of the said Council, number nineteen, passed on the fifteenth day of december one thousand eight hundred and sixty-eight and intituled " *By-Law to prohibit the keeping of pigs within certain Sections of the City of Montreal*" ; the By-Law of the said Council, Chapter twenty eight passed on the tenth day of may one thousand eight hundred and sixty-five and intituled " *By-Law concerning Sewers*" ; the By-Law of the said Council, number fifteen, passed on the twentieth day of may. one thousand eight hundred and sixty-eight and intituled " *By-Law concerning Scavengers*" ; the By-Law of the said Council, Chapter thirty passed on the tenth day of may, one thousand eight hundred and sixty five and intituled " *By-Law concerning sidewalks*"; the By-Law of the said Council Chapter twenty nine, passed on the tenth day of may, one thousand eight hundred and sixty-five and intituled " *By-Law Concerning streets* ": the By-Law of the said Council Chapter thirty-one passed on the tenth day of may, one thousand eight hundred and sixty-five and intituled " *By-Law concerning Vaults and Cisterns* ;" the By-Law of the said Council, Chapter thirty two passed on the tenth day of may, one thousand eight hundred and sixty five and intituled " *By-Law concerning vehicles* "; the By-Law of the said Council Chapter five passed on the tenth day of may, one thousand eight hundred and sixty-five and intituled " *By law to provide for the care and management of the Montreal water works, and to establish a tariff of water rates,*—shall be and the same are hereby severally repealed : Provided, that such repeal shall not affect any act done or any right accruing or accrued, or established, or any suit, action or proceeding had or commenced in any civil case before the time when said repeal shall take effect, nor any offense committed, nor any penalty or forfeiture incurred, nor any suit or prosecution pending at the time of such repeal, for any offense committed, or for the recovery of any penalty, forfeiture, taxes, rates or assessments incurred or due under any of the By-laws so repealed.

No. 5ა.

By-law for the Inspection of Boilers.

[Passed 16th March 1870.]

Sec. 1.—A competent and skilled person shall be appointed by this Council under the title of " Inspector of Boilers," whose duty it shall be to make inspection of, examine and test Steam Boilers used or employed within the City limits, or to be hereafter used and employed therein, as hereinafter provided; but no person shall be appointed to such office unless he is the holder of a certificate of competency as Engineer of the first class, granted by the Board of Inspectors constituted in virtue of the 31st Victoria, chap. 65, of the Dominion Parliament. *Inspector of Boilers to be appointed.*

Sec. 2.—No person or persons, Company or Corporation, shall hereafter use or employ any Boiler for the generation of steam, or for heating purposes, in public or private buildings, when the pressure used exceeds five pounds per square inch, until the same shall have been first duly examined and tested by the said Inspector, and until the said Inspector shall have furnished to such person or persons, Company or Corporation, a certificate to the effect that the same is constructed in the manner hereinafter provided; and it shall be the duty of the said Inspector to examine and test once in every year all Steam Boilers, as aforesaid, within the City, and to grant to any person or persons, Company or Cor- *No boilers to be used unless inspected* poration, using or employing any such Steam Boiler, a certificate of such annual inspection and examination, if he approves of such Steam Boiler.

Boilers how tested.

Sec. 3.—The Inspector shall subject such Steam Boiler to a test by hydrostatic pressure, the limit of which shall in no case exceed one hundred and fifty pounds to the square inch, and shall, before the Boilers are set in or encased with brick or other material, satisfy himself, by examination and experimental trials, that such Boilers are in each case well made, and of good and suitable material; and in subjecting such Steam Boilers to hydrostatic pressure the said Inspector shall assume one hundred pounds to the square inch as the maximum pressure allowable as a working-power for a new Boiler forty-two inches in diameter, made of the best refined iron, at least one quarter of an inch thick, and shall rate the working pressure of all Boilers, whether of greater or less diameter, according to this standard; and in each case the test applied shall conform to and be indicated by the working pressure desired by the proprietor, within the limit above prescribed as the standard for all such Boilers, and in the ratio of one hundred and fifty pounds to one hundred of working pressure, using the water in such tests at a temperature not exceeding sixty degrees Farenheit. The said Inspector shall have access to all Boilers subject to inspection at all seasonable hours.

Valves.

Sec. 4.—No valve, under any circumstances, shall at any time be so loaded or managed as to subject a Boiler to a greater presure than that allowed by the Inspector, at the then last inspection thereof, as the working pressure; and each Boiler shall have a locked-up valve loaded to such pressure; which said valve shall not be accessible to the proprietor, but to the said inspector only, whose duty it shall be to examine and test the same at least twice a year, of which he shall keep a record.

Sec. 5.—No Boiler or Pipe shall be approved which is made, in whole or in part, of bad material or is unsafe in its form, or dangerous from defective workmanship, age, use, or any other cause. *(Boilers disapproved in certain cases.)*

Sec. 6.—Each Boiler shall be provided with suitable water and pressure guages, and with safety valves of suitable dimensions, sufficient in number, well arranged, and in good working order, and so constructed as to open at or below the working pressure above mentioned. *(Safety valves.)*

Sec. 7.—The said Inspector shall be entitled to ask and receive, from any person or persons, Company or Corporation, using or employing a Steam Boiler or Boilers, as aforesaid, for his first inspection of the same and certificate, the following fees, viz: *(Fees.)*

1.—For a Boiler used for motive power, or manufacturing purposes, *Three Dollars*; provided that if there be more than one Boiler in the same establishment, there shall be charged *Three Dollars* for the first, and *Two Dollars* for every additional boiler used.

2.—For a Boiler used for heating purposes in public buildings, *Two Dollars*.

3.—For a Boiler used for heating purposes in private dwellings, with a pressure as herein before limited, *One Dollar*.—For every subsequent annual or other inspection of such Boilers, by the said Inspector, and certificate, the same fees shall be charged and paid as above specified—all of which fees shall be paid over and accounted for by the said Inspector to the City Treasurer, monthly, or oftener if required.

Inspector under whose control.

Sec. 8.—The said Inspector shall be under the control of the said Council, and shall make a report to the said Council at the end of every year, giving full particulars of the work performed by him as such Inspector, and the various amounts received in his said capacity.

Penalty.

Sec. 9.—Any person or persons, Company or Corporation, using or employing a Steam Boiler, contrary to the provisions of this By law, or not procuring the required certificate, or violating any other provision of this By-law, shall be liable to a fine not exceeding Twenty Dollars, and to an imprisonment not exceeding thirty days, for each offence.

CATALOGUE OF THE CITY GOVERNMENT.

(CONTINUED.)

1866.

HENRY STARNES, Esq., *Mayor.*

ALDERMEN.

F. Contant,	J. B. Rolland,
D. Gorrie,	A. A. Stevenson,
F. David,	W. Rodden,
Geo. Bowie,	Thos. McCready

J. B. Goyette.

COUNCILLORS.

D. McNevin, (1)	B. Bastien,
T. S. Higginson,	J. O. Mercier,
J. W. McGauvran,	B. Devlin,
P. Donovan,	L. Labelle,
Jos. Poupart,	J. Leduc,
A. W. Ogilvie,	M. Lanctot,
David Brown,	A. Bernard,
J. H. Isaacson,	J. E. Mullin, (2)
F. Cassidy,	F. X. St. Charles,

1867.

HON. HENRY STARNES, *Mayor.*

ALDERMEN.

D. Gorrie,	N. Valois,
W. Rodden,	A. W. Ogilvie,
Thos. McCready,	B. Devlin,
F. David,	B. Bastien,

Jos. Poupart.

(1). Resigned July 1866 and replaced by W. Masterman.
(2). Unseated by judgment of the Court and replaced by Chs. Alexander, January 1867.

COUNCILLORS.

David Brown,
J. H. Isaacson,
F. Cassidy,
L. O. Mercier,
L. Labelle,
J. Leduc,
M. Lanctôt, (1)
A. Bernard,
F. X. St. Charles,

Chs. Alexander,
J. W. McGauvran,
W. Masterman,
R. Holland,
H. A. Nelson,
R. Taylor,
Jos. Doutre,
D. Munro,
James McShane, (2)

1868.

WILLIAM WORKMAN, Esq., *Mayor.*

ALDERMEN.

W. Rodden,
T. McCready,
F. David,
N. Valois,

B. Devlin,
Chs. Alexander,
A. Bernard,
B. Bastien,

D. Munro.

COUNCILLORS.

J. Leduc,
F. X. St. Charles,
J. W. McGauvran,
W. Masterman,
R. Holland,
H. A. Nelson,
R. Taylor,
Jos. Doutre,
A. Dubord,

James McShane,
T. Wilson,
Henry Lyman,
R. H. Stephens,
T. M. Thomson,
G. W. Stephens,
W. Henderson,
Jos. Simard,
P. Jordan, (3)

(1). Unseated by judgement of the Court and replaced by Alexis Dubord, June 1867.
(2). Replaced P. Donavan, resigned, march 1867.
(3). Replaced L. Labelle, deceased.

CATALOGUE OF THE CITY GOVERNMENT. 247

1869.

WILLIAM WORKMAN, Esq., Mayor.

ALDERMEN.

F. David,
N. Valois,
B. Bastien,
D. Munro,
W. Rodden,
B. Devlin,
A. Bernard,
Chs. Alexander,
W. Masterman.

COUNCILLORS.

J. W. McGauvran,
H. A. Nelson,
R. Taylor,
J. Doutre,
J. McShane,
T. Wilson,
Henry Lyman,
R. H. Stephens,
T. M. Thomson.
Geo. W. Stephens
W. Henderson,
Jos. Simard,
Joel Leduc,
F. X. St. Charles,
P. Jordan,
J. A. Plinguet,
W. F. Kay,
P. M. Christie, 1)

1870.

WILLIAM WORKMAN, Esq. Mayor.

ALDERMEN.

B Bastien,
W. Rodden,
B. Devlin,
A. Bernard,
C. Alexander,
F. David,
W. Masterman,
Thos. Wilson,
Jos. Simard.

COUNCILLORS.

J. McShane,
Henry Lyman,
J. A. Plinguet
W. F. Kay,

(1). Replaced R. Holland, resigned. April 1869.

CATALOGUE OF THE CITY GOVERNMENT.

R. H. Stephens,
T. M. Thomson,
Geo. W. Stephens,
W. Henderson,
Joël Leduc,
F. X. St. Charles,
P. Jordan,

J. W. McGauvran,
H. A. Nelson,
R. Taylor,
P. M. Christie,
L. Betournay,
S. Rivard,
C. Desmarteau,

LIST OF ACTING MAYORS.

(CONTINUED)

J. Leduc. Esquire	12th June	1865.
A. McGibbon "	11th Sept	"
F. Cassidy "	11th Dec	"
J W McGauvran"	12th March	1866
F. X. St Charles "	11th June	"
A. W. Ogilvie "	10th Sept	"
J. O. Mercier "	10th Dec	"
D. Brown "	11th March	1867
B. Bastien "	11th June	"
Chs. Alexander "	9th Sept	"
N. Valois "	9th Dec	"
W. Masterman "	9th March	1868
J. Doutre "	8th June	"
J. McShane "	14th Sept	"
J. Simard "	14th Dec	"
H. A. Nelson "	8th March	1869
D. Munro "	14th June	"
R. H. Stephens "	13th Sept	"
T. Wilson "	13th Dec	"
G. W. Stephens "	14th March	1870

OFFICERS OF THE CORPORATION.

John P. Sexton, City Recorder.
Chs. Glackmeyer, City Clerk.
James F. D. Black, City Treasurer.
P. Macquisten, City Surveyor.
Patrick O'Meara, Assistant City Clerk
Wm. Robb, City Auditor.
Louis Lesage, Superintendent Water Works.
Charles Lapierre, Accountant Water Works.
F. W. L. Penton, Chief of Police.
H. I. Ibbotson, Clerk Recorder's Court.
A. Bertram, Chief Engineer Fire Department.
Wm. Patton, Assistant- do
O. Rouillard, Inspector of Buildings.
A. R. Sowdon, Deputy City Surveyor.
Jos. Smith, Engineer and Draughtsman, City Surveyor's Office,
John O'Connor, G. E. Starnes, D. Clarihue, and W. A. Mussen, Clerks, Treasurers's Office.
W. Lane, F. X. Castonguay, W. D. McNeill, D. McLean and John Palmer, Extra Clerks do.
C. Perrin, Jas. O'Brien, Paul Lefort and Henry Filteau, Clerks Water Works Office.
P. N. Lamothe and P. J. Curran, Clerks in the City Surveyor's Office.
J. V. Duverger, Extra Clerk Recorder's Court.
F. H. Badger, Chief Telegraph Operator.
F. X. Gauthier and James Yuill Assist. Telegraph operators.
J. Perrigo, Clerk Bonsecours Market
F. Benoit, Assistant   do.

OFFICERS OF THE CORPORATION.

Henry Kollmyer, Clerk of St. Ann's Market.
Thomas Day, Assistant   do.
Joseph Robillard, Clerk of Cattle Market.
F. X. Payette, Assistant   do.
A. Schwartz, Clerk of Hay Market.
Wm. Monahan, Assistant   do.
Wm. Gunn, Clerk of St. Lawrence Market.
T. Orsali, Clerk of Papineau Market
M. M. Vaughan, Clerk of St. Gabriel Market.
Ed. Payette, Clerk of St. Antoine Market.
A. D. Joubert, Jos. Dumont, L. C. Therien and I. Ringuette, Bailiffs.
James Darcy, Messenger,

    HENRY STUART, ROUER ROY, *Attorneys*

      W. ROSS, and C. F. PAPINEAU, *Notaries.*

BOARD OF ASSESSORS.

James C. Beers,	P. H. Morin,
J. B. Allard,	David Brown,
W. Douglas,	J. T. Dillon,

CLERKS

F. L. Coursol,	Jos. Bouchard,

      W. O. FARMER

INDEX.

ALARM TELEGRAPH......................134, 172
ALBERT—Street opened........................... 85
ANIMALS.
    Cruelty to.. 139
    Dead 150, 187
ARREST.
    Of persons voting illegally.............. 36, 87
ASSESSMENT.
    Special for local improvements...... 16, 17, 41
    For sidewalks....................................... 30
    For schools 97
ASHES... 168
AUDITOR—City............................... 15, 99
AWNINGS.. 201
BALCONIES 116
BATHING... 139
BEAMS—or supporters 120
BILLARDS—Tax on................................ 109
BOARD OF CHAIRMEN.
    On tavern certificate....................26, 37
BOARD OF HEALTH............................. 140
BOILERS—Steam................................... 241
BREAD 111
BROKERS—Tax on................................. 107
BUILDINGS.
    Erection of... 114
    Parties intending to build, shall give
        notice 198
    Building materials.............................. 198
    May be demolished at fires................. 171

INDEX.

Old and unsafe................................ 49, 122
CARRIAGES.
    Hackney... 210
    Carts, trucks, &c............................... 217
    Carriages in general......................... 221
CARTERS—By-law relating to.................... 210
CATTLE.
    Running at large.............................. 174
CARDS.
    Playing at...................................... 138
CHIMNEYS.
    Construction of........................117, 118
    Sweeping of.................................... 169
CITY AUDITOR.................................. 15, 99
CITY TREASURER—Absence provided for... 14
CITY PASSENGER RAILWAY.................... 86
CLOSING HOURS.
    For taverns, &c.....................43, 75, 108
COAL.. 125
COAL OIL... 160
COMMISSIONERS.
    In cases of expropriation............... 16, 17
    Their qualification........................... 41
    For the Park................................... 46
CONSOLIDATED FUND.
    With classes A.B.C. stock....20, 21, 22, 24, 38, 39
CRUELTY.
    To animals..................................... 139
DEAD.
    Animals...................................150, 187
    Bodies not to be transported in covered carriages...................................... 222

DELAY.
    Within which real estate may be sold for taxes............ 18
DIRTY WATER 140
DISCOUNT.
    On water rates............ 81, 82
DISQUALIFICATION.
    Of members............ 14
DOGS............ 127
DOOR STEPS............ 193
DOORS.
    Of public buildings to open exteriorly... 123
DRAINS—See Sewers
DRILL SHED.
    Loan for............ 9
EDUCATION.
    Extracts from Act............ 51, 73
ELECTION.
    Of members, time altered............ 12
    Illegal voting at, penalty for............ 36, 37
ENCUMBERING—Streets, &c............ 189
ENCLOSURE—Of vacant lots............ 146
EXPROPRIATION.
    Majority of proprietors may object..15, 16, 25
    Plan not required............ 17
    Commissioners to make out special assessment, &c............ 16
    In case of amicable arrangement a special sessment to be made............ 17
    Commissioners to determine first who are the parties interested,............ 25
    In connection with the general plan of the City............ 39

INDEX.

What? where there is but a small depth of the lot after expropriation 40
Prothonotary to remit interest on deposits &c. 40
Commissioners',—property qualification. 41
Rolls of assessment may be annulled and others ordered, &c. 41

FARMERS.
Licensed to sell potatoes by the bag, &c. 92

FIRE ARMS 169
FIRE COMMISSIONERS 70
FIRE DEPARTMENT 131
FIRE MARSHAL 65, 70
FIREWOOD 136
FIREWORKS 169

FOOTPATHS.
Assessment for 30

FRANCHISE.
Extended 12, 13

GARDENERS.
Licensed to sell potatoes by the bag, &c. 92

GAMING 138, 139
GOOD MORALS—and decency 138
GRATINGS 203
HAY MARKET 88

HEADS OF DEPARTMENTS.
To furnish statement of appropriation required 102

HEARTH STONES 110

HOSE
Penalty against persons injuring 133

HOT AIR.
Furnaces 162

Registers 164
HOURS.
    Of closing taverns, &c 43, 75, 76, 108
HOUSES.
    Of ill fame 44
    To be numbered 206
HUCKSTERS.
    Provisions relating to, repealed 93
HYDRANTS 230
INNKEEPERS 26, 37, 43, 75, 108
INSPECTOR.
    Of Boilers 241
    Of Bread 112
    Of Firewood 136
    Of Buildings 113, 122
    May order demolition of buildings in certain cases 49, 122
INTEREST.
    On stock, Debentures, &c 39
    On arrears of assessments 81, 82
JUNK STORES 48
JURORS AND JURIES 58
LAMP POSTS 205
LIGHTING 205
LITTLE ST. JAMES.
    Street, change of level 94, 103
LIVERY STABLES—Tax on 107
LOAN
    Of $75,000 (drainage) 8, 9
    Of $75,000 (Drill Shed) 9
    Of $200,000 (Water Works) 9
    Of $250,000 (City Hall) 28
    Of $400,000 (Consolidation) 18, 19

LOAN
    Of $175,005 (Water Works).......... 19
    Of $300,000 (Mount Royal Park)...... 44 45
    Of $500,000 (Water Works).................. 46
MATCHES........ 167
METRES—(Water)................................ 237
MEETINGS.
    Special—how called............ .... 5, 6
MILK.
    Sale of.. 48, 144
MOUNT ROYAL PARK........................... 44
MUSICAL SALOONS................................ 139
NEW CITY HALL..................................... 28
NOTRE DAME STREET.
    Widening of................... 6, 7, 83, 90, 93
NUISANCES... 146
OBSTRUCTIONS.
    In Streets, &c........ 189
OIL FACTORIES...................................... 157
OLD WALLS. 122
PARK.
    Mount-Royal......... 44
    Commissioners......... .... ,........... 45
PARTITION WALLS................................ 121
PAVING STREETS................................... 30
PEACE—And good order....................... 172
PETROLEUM....... ,......... 160
PIGS—Keeping of..................... 30, 178
PLACARDS—Posting of......... 206
PLAN—Not required in certain cases............ 17
POLICE FORCE.
    At criminal Courts......,........................... 72
PRIVIES.... .... 116, 151

INDEX.

PROTHONOTARY.
    To remit interest on deposits.............. 40
POUNDS—Public.................................. 173
QUALIFICATION.
    Of voters... 12, 13
    Of members....................................... 13, 14
REAL ESTATE.
    May be sold for taxes........................ 18
RECORDER'S COURT.
    Certain proceedings simplified............. 7
    Oral evidence allowed in certain cases. 7, 8
    Penalties, when not paid..................... 8
    Clerk to conduct cases, &c.................. 8
    Recording proceedings simplified......... 27
    Depositions in certain cases need not be
        in writing...................................... 27
    Name in which certain prosecutions may
        be instituted.................................. 42
    One third of certain penalties to
        go to Prov. Govt........................... 42
    Imprisonment in case of non payment
        of fine... 42
    Penalties for infractions of By-Laws...... 43
    Punishment of persons frequenting disor-
        derly houses................................. 44
    Certain provisions, not to apply to cri-
        minal procedure........................... 44
RELIGIOUS WORSHIP—Not to be molested.. 172
REPEAL—of By-laws................................ 237
RESERVOIRS—Not to be interfered with...... 231
RETURNING OFFICERS.
    Absence of, provided for..................... 20
RIOTS.. 172

ROOFING—Composition 115
ROOFS—Snow on 196
SALE OF PROPERTY—For taxes, &c 18
SCAVENGERS 154, 155, 184
SCHOOL.
    Tax 52, 97
    Commissioners may effect loans 57, 73
SEWERS.
    Construction of 179
    Cost, by whom borne 179
    Private 180
    Connections 182, 183
SHAVINGS 167
SIDEWALKS 30, 188, 194, 195
SIGNAL BOXES 135
SIGNS 201
SINKING FUND 23, 24, 25
SCAFFOLDS 122
SLAUGHTER HOUSES 157, 162
SNOW.
    Removal of 194, 196
SOAP FACTORIES 149, 157, 162
SPECIAL MEETINGS—how called 5, 6
SPOUTS 119
STABLES 27, 77, 78
STAGNANT WATER 120
STEAM.
    Engines 157, 162
    Boilers 241
ST. FELIX STREET.
    Discontinued in part 85

STOCK BOOK.
    To be kept by City Treasurer.............. 22
STOVES.
    In partitions, regulated....... 120
STOVE PIPES.................................... 118, 166
STREETS.
    Paving of, may be assessed................ 30
    Under whose superintendence.............. 196
    Width of.................... 196
    May be closed to allow certain works being made.. 197
    Precautions to be taken for excavations.. 197
    Allotment to be made by surveyor for building materials........................ 198
    Preparing mortar, &c., in, prohibited..... 200
    Placing coal or firewood in, regulated..... 200
    Doors to archways to open inwards....... 200
    Signs................. 201
    Awnings 201
    Wares suspended from houses.............. 201
    Raising goods from, by tackle.............. 202
    Crossings 202
    Apertures, coal holes, &c...... 203
    Coal holes and gratings 203
    Earth not to be removed without permission 204
    Pavement and sidewalks, injury to....... 204
    Boundary stones................................ 204
    Trees............................. .... 204, 205
    Certain games in, prohibited 205
    Numbering of houses........................... 206
SUNDAY
    Observance of............................. 82, 138

TARIFF.
- Water Rates 233
- Carriages 216

TAVERN KEEPERS............ 26, 37, 43, 75, 108
TANNERIES 157, 162
TRANSFERS—Of stock............................ 38
TREES—Planting of, in streets........... 48, 104, 194
VACANT LOTS—.............................. 146, 147
VARNISH FACTORIES............................ 157
VAULTS AND CISTERNS........................ 206
VEHICLES
- Hackney carriages........................... 210
- Carts, trucks &.............................. 217
- Vehicles in general......................... 221

VOTING—illegal-punishable..................... 36
WALLS—partition................................. 121
- Dilapidated................................... 122

WATER RATES
- Established................................... 233
- Discount on............................. 81, 82

WATER WORKS..................................... 229
- Introduction of pipes in buildings......... 229
- How laid-when building is distant from line of street................................ 30
- Supply may be cut off...................... 232
- Reservoirs................................... 231
- Metres....................................... 237

WOODEN BUILDINGS............................. 114
WOOD YARDS..................................... 168
YARDS—to be kept clean......................... 149

www.ingramcontent.com/pod-product-compliance
Lightning Source LLC
Chambersburg PA
CBHW032142230426
43672CB00011B/2427